How to Enhance Your Wealth Today

The Book on Discovering Financial Success

Carlos Portillo

ISBN: 978-1-77277-066-7

Published by
10-10-10 Publishing
Markham, Ontario
CANADA

Contents

Dedication

I would like to dedicate this book to you, my reader, for your interest in gaining more knowledge to enhance your wealth. As of now, you may not have the tools and techniques to improve your financial well-being, but you will learn them through the process of reading this book.

I acknowledge and applaud your willingness to think about your future and make a difference in the way you can manage your finances more effectively.

Also, I dedicate this book to my mother, Lucia, who taught me that hard work and tenacity are the foundation of success.

Finally, this book is dedicated to my wife Maria Teresa and my children Carlos Jr., Ana Lucia, and Maria Fernanda, for their support during my professional journey and their patience during those long working hours.

Acknowledgments

I am deeply honoured to have around me family, friends, mentors, teachers, and colleagues who have made great contributions in my life.

I thank my university professors for teaching me the foundation of my career. Without them I would not be able to succeed in my professional field.

I thank my managers and mentors during my professional journey since they shared with me the leadership skills necessary to become a great manager.

I thank my friends, Francisco, Ernesto, Ivan, who helped during my time of thinking and taking my next steps as a finance professional.

About the Author

Carlos Portillo started working for corporations since he was in 4th. Year of High-School. After almost three decades of working he has learned a number of tools and systems from corporations and from his continuous formal training from professional associations and applied such learnings in his day-to-day personal life which had helped him to enhance his wealth is a short period of time. Carlos is avid in sharing such learnings with family and friends so they can improve their wealth.

Foreword

Carlos Portillo is an extremely successful finance professional. Over the last 25 years, he has learned about the different tools and techniques that allow corporations to succeed and become sustainable in the long term. He has applied such learning in his personal life and has been able to improve his well-being in a holistic way at different stages of his life; as a father, husband, friend, and citizen.

In this book, *How to Enhance Your Wealth Today*, Carlos has incorporated the tools and techniques that will help you to enhance your financial well-being, bring peace of mind for your future, and relieve you of the struggles and stress in your day-to-day living. In modern life, financial stress can be the root cause of different unfortunate events such as divorce, bankruptcy, children not receiving post secondary school education and losing your home; among others. I recommend this book as a definite must read as Carlos teaches you how you can avoid encountering such circumstances within these very pages.

Carlos Portillo

Carlos connects the dots and demonstrates how you too can enhance your wealth by applying his valuable financial concepts today!

Raymond Aaron
New York Times Bestselling Author

Introduction

Your Transcendental Purpose

Time is a resource you can't buy. I've been working as a finance professional for large companies since I was 17. As most of the middle class professionals, I started my career at the bottom of the organizational structure, by working and studying very hard to strengthen my skills and experience in order to make a difference in both my personal development and the companies I've worked for. In the winter of 2016, and after working for almost three decades, I decided to take a break from the work-force and spend time with my family, siblings, nephews, nieces, and some friends that I rarely had the opportunity to spend time with due to my day-to-day responsibilities. During this time of interaction with all the people around me I found that one of the factors they all have in common is their challenges to improve their financial well-being and, for some others, the struggle to cover the basic monthly bills. Another important aspect they have in common though, and one that I believe is the most relevant, is their passion to contribute to our society by being and forming good citizens (their children), working hard, making this country a better place to live in, and transmitting their dreams and vision to the younger generations. This is what I call "The Transcendental Purpose."

During my interaction with friends, colleagues, neighbours, and my own family, all of them in different age groups, sadly I noticed some of my baby boomers' friends won't have enough savings to keep the post-retirement lifestyle they wish to have. Some others want to be remembered by their children and grandchildren based on a legacy they wish they could leave to them but won't be able to. Some of my friends from generation X and Y are not maximizing the generous tax deferral and saving programs from the government. They are not managing their cash flow effectively so they can't support their children with post-secondary education or saving for an emergency fund. And last but not least, the young adults, including my children and their friends, are accumulating a huge debt to pay for their university studies (and travel, which is not a wise decision).

After reflecting on all the experiences I had from interacting with all these people around me I thought… How can I help them? How can I help other people living with the same financial struggles and challenges? So I decided to write this book. In this book I share concepts and tools used by successful corporations, and their application to individuals and families to "Enhance their Wealth Today." Saving,Investing, and Growth are impacted by three variables: capital, rate of return, and TIME.

Time is precious and is a resource one can't buy; therefore, it is important to take action TODAY. Enhance your wealth TODAY with this book.

Chapter 1

Understanding Generational Differences

In the last decade, University of Maryland Psychology Professor Ruth F. Fassinger, PhD, has observed several differences in the work habits of younger and older women in interviews she's conducted with more than 100 prominent women across an array of occupational fields. In particular, the younger women tend to more often question workplace expectations, such as long work hours or taking work home, and they often are more open about their parenting obligations and commitments.

Some studies suggest that such differences are, in part, accounted for by workers' values shifting as they age. For example, business-management researchers Karen Wey Smola and Charlotte D. Sutton, PhD, surveyed 350 baby boomers and gen Xers in 1974 and 1999 and found an overall change in work values as generations matured, such as giving work a lower priority in life and placing less value in feeling a sense of pride at work.

Generational differences sometimes may cause clashes in the workplace, especially among workers on teams, Patterson notes. For example, she says, boomers may believe gen Xers are too impatient and willing to throw out the tried-and-true strategies, while gen Xers may view boomers as always trying to say the right thing to the right person and being inflexible to change. Traditionalists may view baby boomers as self-absorbed and prone to sharing too much information, and baby boomers may view traditionalists as dictatorial and rigid. And, gen Xers may consider millennials too spoiled and self-absorbed, while millennials may view gen Xers as too cynical and negative.[1]

In terms of dealing with money, baby boomers may have the practice of "Buy now, pay later" while generations Xers may be more cautious and conservative and young adults would "Earn to spend." A lack of understanding across generations can have detrimental effects on communication, working relationships and dealing with money behaviours that undermine effective and proactive preservation of wealth. In this chapter I will cover the three main generational groups, including some of most relevant behaviours and preferences so you may identify yourself with such behaviours but, most importantly, so you will learn how to Enhance your Wealth, taking advantage of behaviours and preferences aligned with your goals.

1.1 Young Adults (Millennials), Generation X, Baby Boomers, and Traditionalists

According to experts, there are 4 main generational groups, with the following birth years:

- Young adults (Millennials): 1977-2000
- Generation X: 1965-1980
- Baby Boomers: 1946-1964
- Traditionalists: 1900-1945

The scope of this book covers the first three groups.

1.2 Influencers

Influencers are global events, trends, and changes that impacted the different generations and revolutionized they way the see the world. For instance, for **Baby Boomers** such events would be: Civil rights, Vietnam war, sexual revolution, Cold War, space travel, highest rate of divorces and 2nd marriages in history. "The American Dream" was promised to them as children and they pursued it. As a result, they are seen as being greedy, materialistic and ambitious.

For **Generations Xers**, events such as the water-gate, energy crisis, dual income families and single parents, first generation of latchkey kids, Y2K, activism, corp. downsizing, end of cold war, mom's work, increased divorce rate. Their perceptions were shaped by growing up having to take care of themselves early and watching their politicians lie and their parents getting laid off.

Came of age when USA was losing its status as the most powerful and prosperous nation in the world. The first generation that will NOT do as well financially as their parents did.

For **Young Adults** (Millennials) such influencers would be: Digital media, child focused world, school shootings, terrorist attacks, AIDS, 9/11 terrorist attacks. Typically grew up as children of divorce and they hope to be the next great generation and to turn around all the "wrong" they see in the world today. They grew up more sheltered than any other generation as parents strived to protect them from the dangers of the world. Came of age in a period of economic expansion and globalization.

1.3 Core Values

The following are some of the core values for each generation: For **Baby Boomers**: Anti war, anti government, anything is possible, equal rights, equal opportunities, extremely loyal to their children (this is why most of the Baby Boomers feel highly committed in leaving a legacy for their children), involvement, optimism, personal gratification, personal growth, question everything, spend now, worry later, team oriented, transformational, want to "make a difference."

For **Generations Xers**: believe in balance, diversity, are entrepreneurial, have fun, are highly educated and have high job expectations. They are Independent, informal and pragmatists. seek life balance, self-reliance, skepticism/cynical, think globally.

For **Millennials**: achievement, avid consumers, civic duty, confidence, diversity, extreme fun, high morals, highly tolerant, hotly competitive, like personal attention, self confident, social ability, members of global community, most educated generation, extremely techno savvy, extremely spiritual, and street smarts among others.

1.4 Attributes

Attributes are the skills and competitive advantages as follows:

For **Baby Boomers**: ability to handle a crisis, ambitious, challenge authority, competent, competitive, consensus leadership, consumerism, ethical, good communication skills, idealism, live to work, loyal to careers and employers, most educated as compared to other 3 generations, multi-taskers, rebellious against convention, traditionally found their worth in their work ethic but now seek a healthy life/work balance, optimistic, political correctness, strong work ethic and willing to take on responsibility.

For **Generations Xers**: adaptable, angry but don't know why, antiestablishment mentality, big gap with boomers, can change, crave independence, confident, competent, ethical, flexible, focus on results, free agents, high degree of brand loyalty, ignore leadership, independent, loyal to manager, pampered by their parents, pragmatic, results driven, self-starters, self sufficient, skeptical of institutions, strong sense of entitlement, unimpressed with authority, willing to take on responsibility, willing to put in the extra time to get a job done, work/\life balance, work to live.

For **Millennials**: Ambitious but not entirely focused, look to the workplace for direction and to help them achieve their goals, ease in teams, attached to their gadgets & parents, best educated – confident, diversity focused – multiculturalism, have not lived without computers, eager to spend money, fiercely independent, focus is children/family, focus on change using technology, friendly, scheduled, structured lives, globalism (global way of thinking), greatly indulged by fun loving parents, heroism - consider parents their heroes, high speed stimulus junkies, incorporate individual, responsible into their jobs, innovative-think out of the box, individualistic yet group oriented, loyal to peers, sociable - makes workplace friends, "me first" attitude in work life, net-centric, team players, open to new ideas, optimistic, parent advocacy (parents are advocates), political savvy (like the Boomers), respect given for competency not title, respectful of character development, self –absorbed, strong sense of entitlement, techno savvy - digital generation, think mature generation is "cool", want to please others, hope to make life contributions to world, seek responsibility early on in their roles.

1.5 Dealing with money

In dealing with money and financial maters Baby Boomers have the fundamental of "Buy Now, Pay Later"; Generation Xers are cautious, conservative and are "Savers" while Millennials want "Earn to Spend"

1.6 Work Ethics

Baby Boomers: Driven, workaholic-60 hr work weeks, work long hours to establish self-worthiness, and identity and fulfillment. work ethic = worth ethic, quality.

Generations Xers: Balance, work smarter and with greater output, not work longer hours, eliminate the task, self-reliant, want structure & direction, skeptical.

Millennials: Ambitious, what's next?, multitasking, tenacity, entrepreneurial.

1.7 View on Work/Life Balance

Baby Boomers: Were hesitant of taking too much time off work for fear of losing their place on the corporate team. As a result, there is an imbalance between work and family.

Generations Xers: Because of parents who are Boomer workaholics, they focus on clearer balance between work and family. Do not worry about losing their place on the corporate team it they take time off.

Millennials: Not only balance with work and life, but balance with work, life and community involvement and self development. flex time, job sharing, and sabbaticals will be requested more by this generation.

1.8 Preferred Work Environment

For **Baby Boomers**: "Flat" organizational hierarchy, democratic, humane, equal opportunity, warm, friendly environment.

For **Generations Xers**: Functional, positive, fun, efficient, fast paced and flexible, informal, access to leadership, access to information.

For **Millennials**: Collaborative, achievement-oriented, highly creative, positive, diverse, fun, flexible, want continuous feedback.

1.9 Mentoring

Baby Boomers: Stellar career important as they question where I have been and where I am going. Appreciate they paid their dues under the hierarchical rules

Teach them balance, work, family, financial, etc.

Need to know they are valued, show them how you can help them, use their time wisely

Pre-assess their comfort level with technology before new projects, demonstrate the importance of a strong team and their role. Emphasize that their decision is a good one and a "victory" for them. Follow up, check in, and ask how the individual is doing on a regular basis, but DO NOT micro-manage.

Generations Xers, Offer a casual work environment&. get them involved, encourage creativity. allow flexibility, be more hands off, encourage a learning environment, listen - and learn! They work with you, not for you, offer variety and stimulation. May need help in taking responsibility for full process completion and in appreciating how their input affects the whole. Need their managers to appreciate that they have a life/can be more efficient one task at a time. They will leave in a second if a better deal comes along. Provide learning and development opportunities. Provide situations to try new things. Ask for their input in selecting an option. Be prepared to answer "why" often present yourself as an information. provider, not boss, use their peers as testimonials. Appear to enjoy your work follow up and meet your commitments. They are eager to improve and expect you to follow through with information.

Millennials: Encouragement to explore new avenues through breaking the rules. Raise the bar on self as they have high expectations. Goals – in steps and actions. Establish mentoring programs. Honor their optimism and welcome and nurture them. Be flexible, challenge them, respect them. Offer customization- a plan specific to them. Offer peer-level examples, spend time providing information and guidance. Allow options, including work from home and flex time. Be impressed with their decisions

1.10 Retirement

Baby Boomers: If I retire, who am I? I haven't saved any money so I need to work, at least part time. I I've been downsized so I need to work, at least part time.

Generations Xers: I may retire early; I've saved my money. I may want different experiences and may change careers. I may want to take a sabbatical to develop myself.

Millennials: Jury is still out but will probably be similar to Gen Xers

Chapter 2

Defining Your Values[2]

In chapter 1 you have learned about the generational strengths and opportunities. You have learned also about core values and attributes for the different generations. In this chapter you will learn about some techniques and tools that will help you with defining your own personal values. Please keep in mind there is no right or wrong priorities or hierarchy of your values, and they may change depending on your own life stage. When you define your personal values, you discover what's truly important to you. A good way of starting to do this is to look back on your life – to identify when you felt really good, and really confident that you were making good choices.

2.1 How would you define your values?

Before you answer this question, you need to know what, in general, values are. Your values are the things that you believe are important in the way you live and work. They (should) determine your priorities and, deep down, they're probably the measures you use to tell if your life is turning out the way you want it to.

When the things that you do and the way you behave match your values, life is usually good – you're satisfied and content. But when these don't align with your personal values, that's when things feel... wrong. This can be a real source of unhappiness. This is why making a conscious effort to identify your values is so important.

2.2 How Values Help You

Values exist, whether you recognize them or not. Life can be much easier when you acknowledge your values – and when you make plans and decisions that honor them.

If you value family, but you have to work 70-hour weeks in your job, will you feel internal stress and conflict? And if you don't value competition, and you work in a highly competitive sales environment, are you likely to be satisfied with your job?

In these types of situations, understanding your values can really help. When you know your own values, you can use them to make decisions about how to live your life, and you can answer questions like these:

- What job should I pursue?
- Should I accept this promotion?
- Should I start my own business?
- Should I compromise, or be firm with my position?
- Should I follow tradition, or travel down a new path?

So, take the time to understand the real priorities in your life, and you'll be able to determine the best direction for you and your life goals.

Values are usually fairly stable, yet they don't have strict limits or boundaries. Also, as you move through life, your values may change. For example, when you start your career, success – measured by money and status – might be a top priority. But after you have a family, work-life balance may be what you value more.

As your definition of success changes, so do your personal values. This is why keeping in touch with your values is a lifelong exercise. You should continuously revisit this, especially if you start to feel unbalanced... and you can't quite figure out why.

As you go through the exercise below, bear in mind that values that were important in the past may not be relevant now.

2.3 Identify the times when you were happiest

Find examples from both your career and personal life. This will ensure some balance in your answers.

What were you doing? Were you with other people? Who? What other factors contributed to your happiness?

2.4 Identify the times when you were most proud

Use examples from your career and personal life.

Why were you proud? Did other people share your pride? Who? What other factors contributed to your feelings of pride?

2.5 Identify the times when you were most fulfilled and satisfied
Again, use both work and personal examples.

What need or desire was fulfilled? How and why did the experience give your life meaning? What other factors contributed to your feelings of fulfillment?

2.6 Determine your top values, based on your experiences of happiness, pride, and fulfillment

Why is each experience truly important an memorable? Use the following list of common personal values to help you get started – and aim for about 10 top values. (As you work through, you may find that some of these naturally combine. For instance, if you value philanthropy, community, and generosity, you might say that service to others is one of your top values.)

Accountability
Accuracy
Achievement
Adventurousness
Altruism
Ambition
Assertiveness
Balance
Being the best
Belonging
Boldness
Calmness
Carefulness
Challenge
Cheerfulness
Clear-mindedness

Commitment
Community
Compassion
Competitiveness
Consistency
Contentment
Continuous Improvement
Contribution
Control
Cooperation
Correctness
Courtesy
Creativity
Curiosity
Decisiveness
Democracy

Dependability	Fluency
Determination	Focus
Devoutness	Freedom
Diligence	Fun
Discipline	Generosity
Discretion	Goodness
Diversity	Grace
Dynamism	Growth
Economy	Happiness
Effectiveness	Hard Work
Efficiency	Health
Elegance	Helping Society
Empathy	Holiness
Enjoyment	Honesty
Enthusiasm	Honor
Equality	Humility
Excellence	Independence
Excitement	Ingenuity
Expertise	Inner Harmony
Exploration	Inquisitiveness
Expressiveness	Insightfulness
Fairness	Intelligence
Faith	Intellectual Status
Family-oriented	Intuition
Fidelity	Joy
Fitness	Justice

How to Enhance Your Wealth Today

Leadership

Legacy

Love

Loyalty

Making a difference

Mastery

Merit

Obedience

Openness

Order

Originality

Patriotism

Perfection

Piety

Positivity

Practicality

Preparedness

Professionalism

Prudence

Quality-oriented

Reliability

Resourcefulness

Restraint

Results-oriented

Rigor

Security

Self-actualization

Self-control

Selflessness

Self-reliance

Sensitivity

Serenity

Service

Shrewdness

Simplicity

Soundness

Speed

Spontaneity

Stability

Strategic

Strength

Structure

Success

Support

Teamwork

Temperance

Thankfulness

Thoroughness

Thoughtfulness

Timeliness

Tolerance

Traditionalism

Trustworthiness	Unity
Truth-seeking	Usefulness
Understanding	Vision
Uniqueness	Vitality

2.7 Prioritize your top values

This step is probably the most difficult, because you'll have to look deep inside yourself. It's also the most important step because, when making a decision, you'll have to choose between solutions that may satisfy different values. This is when you must know which value is more important to you.

Write down your top values, not in any particular order.

Look at the first two values and ask yourself, "If I could satisfy only one of these, which would I choose?" It might help to visualize a situation in which you would have to make that choice. For example, if you compare the values of service and stability, imagine that you must decide whether to sell your house and move to another country to do valuable foreign aid work, or keep your house and volunteer to do charity work closer to home.

Keep working through the list, by comparing each value with each other value, until your list is in the correct order.

2.8 Reaffirm your values

Check your top-priority values, and make sure they fit with your life and your vision for yourself.

Do these values make you feel good about yourself? Are you proud of your top three values? Would you be comfortable and proud to tell your values to people you respect and admire?

Do these values represent things you would support, even if your choice isn't popular, and it puts you in the minority?

When you consider your values in decision making, you can be sure to keep your sense of integrity and what you know is right, and approach decisions with confidence and clarity. You'll also know that what you're doing is best for your current and future happiness and satisfaction.

Making value-based choices may not always be easy. However, making a choice that you know is right is a lot less difficult in the long run.

Key Points

Identifying and understanding your values is a challenging and important exercise. Your personal values are a central part of who you are – and who you want to be. By becoming more aware of these important factors in your life, you can use them as a guide to make the best choice in any situation.

Some of life's decisions are really about determining what you value most. When many options seem reasonable, it's helpful and comforting to rely on your values – and use them as a strong guiding force to point you in the right direction.

Chapter 3

Learning the Financial Basics

Personal finance comprises a broad range of topics such as creating a budget, saving for retirement, and using credit wisely. Understanding the basics of money management will allow you to live well today and build a strong financial future. In this chapter you will learn the aspects and the tools to build your financial plan.

3.1 Financial Planning

The big picture: your financial plan

Seeing the big picture can help you reach your financial goals. Professionals can help you create your plan.

Financial planning means creating a long-term vision and clear goals for the future you want. Creating a financial plan helps you see what you're trying to achieve and how all of the major pieces of your financial world add up to one complete picture relative to your goals.

Major pieces of your financial plan include:

- Your job, your career, or business
- Your spending plan
- Your bank accounts
- Major assets you own
- Debts you owe
- Real estate
- Insurance
- Investments
- Estate planning for the next generation

Take advantage of professional advice. Some financial services companies will answer basic financial questions for free, or create a basic financial plan for as little as a few hundred dollars. You may have to pay for some planning services, but financial advice doesn't have to be expensive.

3.2 Tax Planning

People and organizations don't think about who is their main stakeholder. From my perspective your main stakeholder is the government, since productive people and organizations must reimburse governments from their profit with let's say 25% to 49% in the form of taxes. That is why tax planning and maximizing tax incentives, deferred tax programs, tax free investment programs, etc. are very important. In this chapter you will learn about the most common tax programs for individuals.

3.3 Canadian Tax System

Most adult Canadians pay taxes, in one form or another. Taxes are paid at all three levels of government: federal, provincial and municipal. The federal tax system is administered by the Canada Revenue Agency (CRA). In addition to collecting taxes on behalf of the federal government, the CRA also collects taxes on behalf of all provinces except Quebec. Municipal taxes are collected at the local level.

Total versus Taxable Income

A person's total income represents the sum of all income from various sources. Some of the major sources of income include employment income, commissions, some government benefits, pension income, various types of investment income, business income, rental income, and taxable benefits received from his or her employer.

An individual's total income is not entirely subject to income taxes. In calculating taxable income, a person is allowed to make certain tax deductions from his or her total income. Some of the major tax deductions include pension plan contributions, RRSP contributions, union dues, child care expenses, support payments, carrying charges, and moving expenses.

In general, taxable income is calculated as follows:

Taxable Income = Total Income - Tax Deductions

Marginal Tax Rate

The marginal tax rate represents the amount of tax an individual pays on his or her next dollar of income. Marginal tax rates are usually presented in a table format. For example, the current marginal tax rates for federal income taxes are as follows:

Taxable Income	Marginal Tax Rates
First $43,561	15%
Over $43,561 up to $87,123	22%
Over $87,123 up to $135,054	26%
Over $135,054	29%

Average Tax Rate

The average tax rate represents how much tax is payable as a percentage of income.

average tax rate = (tax payable ÷ taxable income) x 100

Federal and Provincial Tax Rates

In addition to federal income taxes, a taxpayer must also pay provincial taxes. In general, the table of marginal tax rates in every province is similar to that of the federal government. That is, as a taxpayer's income increases, the amount of income tax they pay on the next dollar of income will progressively increase. This is referred to as a progressive income tax system.

The only exception is Alberta where a flat tax of 10% is applied to all taxable income.

Tax Deductions versus Tax Credits

Tax deductions reduce the amount of income on which an individual pays taxes. On the other hand, a tax credit reduces the amount of tax payable. Tax credits are applied after all tax deductions have been made and tax payable has been calculated using the combined federal and provincial marginal tax rates. Tax credits can be used to reduce the federal tax payable and the provincial tax payable.

average tax rate = (tax payable ÷ taxable income) x 100

A tax deduction will reduce taxable income, the denominator. A tax credit will reduce tax payable, the numerator. In either case, the average tax rate will decrease.

Carlos Portillo

Types of Tax Credits

There are two types of tax credits:
- refundable
- non-refundable

Refundable credits are tax credits that are paid directly to an individual, if they are not needed to reduce his or her tax payable. For example, Peter has $600 in taxes owing and a refundable tax credit of $1000, he will receive a $400 refund from the CRA, calculated as $1000 - $600. The most common refundable tax credit is the GST tax credit.

Non-refundable credits are tax credits that can only be used to reduce the tax payable. Once an individual has no tax payable, certain non-refundable tax credits may be transferred or carried forward to future tax years. The table below lists those non-refundable tax credits that may be transferred to other individuals, usually a spouse or blood relative, or carried forward by the individual.

Transferable Tax Credits	Tax Credits Eligible for Carry Forward
- Tuition, education and textbook amount - Pension income amount - Age amount - Disability amount	- Medical expenses amount - Tuition, education and textbook amount - Charitable contribution amount

Other Non-Refundable Tax Credits

Some other common federal and provincial non-refundable tax credits include:

- Basic personal amount
- Spouse or common-law partner amount
- Amount for an eligible dependant
- CPP contributions
- Employment insurance premiums
- Canada employment amount
- Public transit amount
- Children's fitness amount
- Interest paid on your student loans

Taxation of Registered and Non-registered Accounts

Registered accounts are savings plans that are defined in the federal Income Tax Act, registered with the Canada Revenue Agency (CRA), and administered by various financial institutions. These types of plans are granted special tax status wherein contributions may be tax deductible and taxes payable on any investment earnings may be deferred. There are also a number of limitations and restrictions on these plans including how withdrawals are treated for tax purposes. The main types of registered accounts are:

- tax-free savings account (TFSA)
- registered education savings plan (RESP)
- registered retirement savings plan (RRSP)
- registered retirement income fund (RRIF)
- registered disability savings plan (RDSP)

Tax Implications

The table below highlights the tax implications of contributions, investment earnings, and withdrawals for these registered accounts.

Type of Account	Contributions are Tax Deductible	Investment Earnings are Taxable Every Year?	Withdrawals are Tax Free?
Tax-free Savings Account (TFSA)	No	No	Yes
Registered Education Savings Plan (RESP)	No	No	Educational Assistance Payments (EAP) withdrawals and withdrawals from the investment returns are taxable; withdrawals of subscriber contributions are tax-free
Registered Retirement Savings Plan (RRSP)	Yes	No	No
Registered Retirement Income Fund (RRIF)	N/A	No	No
Registered Disability Savings Plan (RDSP)	No	No	Disability Assistance Payments (DAP) withdrawals and withdrawals from the investment returns are taxable; withdrawals of contributor contributions are tax-free

There are no particular tax benefits associated with non-registered accounts. Contributions are not tax-deductible and investors must pay tax on the plan's investment income as they earn it. As a tax planning strategy I would recommend individuals maximize RRSP contributions and then, if any income surplus, maximize TFSAs savings.

Types of Income

Depending on the types of investments held within a registered or non-registered account, the types of income that may be earned include the following:

- interest income
- Canadian dividend income
- other income, such as income from foreign property
- capital gains or losses

Interest Income

Interest income refers to investment income that is earned on: 1) cash that is deposited in a chequing or savings account, and 2) various types of debt securities, such as treasury bills (T-Bills), Canada Savings Bonds, term deposits, and guaranteed investment certificates (GICs). Interest income is fully taxed at the investor's top marginal tax rate. In addition, the tax payable on interest income is due in the year in which it is earned.

Dividend Income

Dividend income refers to investment income that is paid out of the after-tax net income of a corporation to its shareholders. Like interest income, the tax payable on dividend income is due in the year in which the dividend is received.

The tax treatment of dividends will depend on the answers to the following questions:

Is the dividend from a Canadian corporation or a foreign corporation?

If the dividend is from a Canadian corporation, is the corporation a large public Canadian corporation or a Canadian–controlled private corporation (CCPC)?

A dividend paid by a foreign corporation is referred to as a foreign dividend and is fully taxable at your top marginal tax rate. A dividend paid by a large public Canadian corporation is referred to as an eligible dividend. A dividend paid by a Canadian-controlled private corporation is referred to as a non-eligible dividend. Eligible and non-eligible dividends are taxed at a lower rate than foreign dividends. The mechanism for this reduced tax payable is referred to as the dividend gross-up and tax credit.

Other Income

Some other types of fully taxable income include:

Interest and dividend income from foreign sources, rental income, partnership income

Spousal support payments, business income, farming income, and fishing income,

Foreign Income

Foreign income is often subject to withholding tax levied by the country in which the income originates. However, the full amount of these earnings must be reported on a Canadian tax return. For Canadian residents, the capital gains tax treatment is the same for foreign and domestic property. Although withholding tax is not applied to capital gains, you may be required to pay tax to the country where your investments are domiciled.

Capital Gains and Losses

A capital asset is any asset that is purchased and maintained for the purpose of generating income. Some examples of capital assets include equipment, buildings, and rental property. A capital gain results when capital assets are sold for more than their cost. Conversely, a capital loss results when capital assets are sold for less than their cost. If capital assets have not been sold, then a capital gain or loss has not been realized; this is referred to as an unrealized capital gain or loss.

- Capital Gain: market price > cost
- Capital Loss: market price < cost

In Canada, only 50% of a capital gain is taxable. This amount is referred to as taxable capital gain. Similarly, only 50% of a capital loss is allowable. This amount is referred to as an allowable capital loss.

For more details on tax matters you can access to the following links and consult with your tax advisor when planning your tax strategies.

Description	URL
Canada: Canada Revenue Agency	cra-arc.gc.ca/menu-eng.html
Alberta: Alberta Treasury Board and Finance	finance.alberta.ca/
British Columbia: Government of British Columbia – Business	gov.bc.ca/en/index.page
Manitoba: Manitoba Taxation Division	gov.mb.ca/finance/index.html
New Brunswick: Government of New Brunswick – Finance	gnb.ca/content/gnb/en/departments/finance.html
Newfoundland: Newfoundland Department of Finance	fin.gov.nl.ca/fin/
Nunavut: Nunavut Department of Finance	finance.gov.nu.ca/
Northwest Territories: Finance	fin.gov.nt.ca/
Nova Scotia: Nova Scotia Department of Finance	novascotia.ca/finance/en/home/default.aspx
Ontario: Ontario Ministry of Finance	fin.gov.on.ca/en/
Prince Edward Island: Department of Finance, Energy and Municipal Affairs	gov.pe.ca/finance/
Quebec: Revenu Quebec	revenuquebec.ca/en/
Saskatchewan: Government of Saskatchewan – Finance	finance.gov.sk.ca/
Yukon: Yukon Department of Finance	finance.gov.yk.ca/

3.4 Building your Budget

What is a budget and why is it important?

Simply put, a budget is an itemized summary of likely income and expenses for a given period. It helps you determine whether you can grab that bite to eat or should head home for a bowl of soup. It is typically created using a spreadsheet, and it provides a concrete, organized, and easily understood breakdown of how much money you have coming in and how much you are letting go. It's an invaluable tool to help you prioritize your spending and manage your money—no matter how much or how little you have.

Planning and monitoring your budget will help you identify wasteful expenditures, adapt quickly as your financial situation changes, and achieve your financial goals. When you actually see the breakdown of your expenses, you may be surprised by what you find; this process is essential to fully grasping how things can add up. Creating a budget will decrease your stress levels because, with a budget, there are no surprises. Unexpected car problems or medical bills? That dream vacation your best friends are planning? With a budget, you don't have to panic or wonder if you have the money—you already know. This sense of financial clarity is important not only in school, but throughout life.

How do I create a budget?

Budgeting is the process of creating a plan to spend your money. Creating this spending plan allows you to determine in advance whether you will have enough money to do the things you need to do or would like to do.

Budgeting is an important planning and forecasting process to help you manage your money by balancing your expenses with your income.

If they don't balance and you spend more than you make, you will have a problem. Many people don't realize that they spend more than they earn and slowly sink deeper into debt every year. If you don't have enough money to do everything you would like to do, then you can use this planning process to prioritize your spending and focus your money on the things that are most important to you.

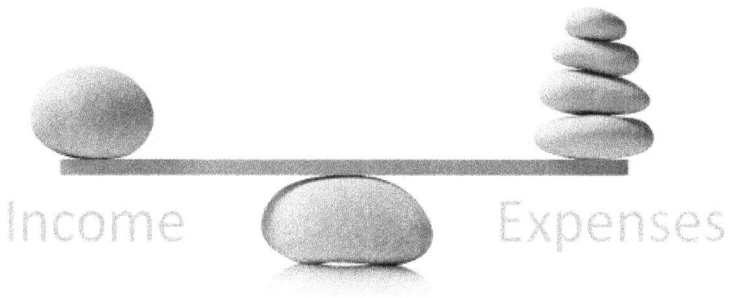

Budgets can be created in an excel file. You should capture the following elements:[3]

1. What are your goals?
2. Where is your money coming from?
3. Where is your money going?
4. Add it all up
5. Make adjustments if needed

1. What are your goals?

The first step in creating a budget is to set your goals. What are your financial goals? Do you have debts you need to pay off? Do you want to minimize the debt you graduate with? Are you trying to save for a car, a vacation, or your future? What do want to accomplish while you are in school and when you graduate? Budgeting involves tough choices, but having a goal will make budgeting a little less painful and allows you to start planning for the future.

Every financial goal you set should be a SMART goal: Specific, Measurable, Achievable, Relevant, and Time Framed.

Your goals can be defined using these three categories:

Short-Term: less than one year
Mid-Term: one to three years
Long-Term: more than five years

For example, let's say that you want to go on a vacation to Europe when you graduate to celebrate your accomplishment! Maybe you are graduating in three years. So you have 36 months to save for your vacation. You did your research and found that you will need to save at least $4,500 for the trip you plan to take. So, that means you will need to set aside $125 each month until you graduate. Guess what? You just created a SMART goal!

Your goal is:

Specific: You plan to go to Europe when you graduate to celebrate your success

Measurable: You know that you will need to save $4,500 to take your trip

Achievable: You will need to save $125 a month to meet your goal

Relevant: Your goal is relevant to you - you plan to take a trip when you graduate as a reward for your hard work

Time-Framed: You plan to reach your goal in 3 years

Now, it's your turn! Think of at least one goal you plan to accomplish using the SMART goal steps.

2. Where is my money coming from?

Where does your money come from? List the sources of your income (e.g., work, student loans, parents) and the amount that comes in from each source each month. If you get one disbursement per semester (e.g., student loans and scholarships), determine the monthly allowance by taking the amount that's left after paying non-recurring costs (e.g., tuition, books, dorm room) and dividing it by the 5 months in a semester.

3. Where is my money going?

Do you check your bank account at the end of the month or semester and wonder where all the money went? Before you can manage your money, you have to know how you're spending it (mortgage, entertainment, child savings, etc.). Use a spreadsheet to track and categorize your expenses for one month. Get in the habit of recording your expenditures once a day.

It's useful to separate your expenses into three categories:

Fixed Needs – Necessary expenses that stay the same from month to month, e.g., rent, phone bill
Variable Needs – Necessary expenses that may vary from month to month, e.g., gas, food
Wants – Non-essential expenses, e.g., lattes, movies, eating out, electronics

If you have a monthly savings goal (and you should!), include it as an expense. It is much easier to save money if you've planned for it in your budget. And it's important, too: if you run into unforeseen expenses, you'll want to be able to pay them without going into debt. And even if nothing goes wrong, having some savings will help you follow your dreams in the future.

4. Add it all up.

When you compare your income and expenses, do you have a monthly surplus, or will you be needing another job and begging your parents for help by the end of the semester?

5. Make adjustments if needed.

If you're over budget, you need a strategy for controlling costs. Balance your budget, starting with the "wants" identified in Step 3.

When you added up your monthly expenses, did you notice any surprisingly large numbers? Did you spend $100 at restaurants or on yet another new outfit? Did you spend more on electronics than food?

Begin with such "wants" that you may be overindulging in. For each type of "want," decide on a reasonable monthly limit that will help you balance your budget. Would it help you reach your goals if you limited yourself to spending $40 a month at restaurants and did more shopping at the grocery store? Can you get by without a monthly clothing or electronics expenditure, making such purchases only after you reach savings goals? Set a cap on your "want" expenses and see if you've balanced your budget.

If you can't trim enough from your "wants" in order to balance your budget, you will need to reduce your variable needs expenditures in the short term and perhaps your fixed needs expenditures in the long term. This may mean taking the bus instead of driving and finding less expensive housing next year.

Yearly Budget Template

This budget template is meant to help you create a budget that works for you. Whether you're saving for your wedding or expecting a new baby, making a budget can help you feel financially prepared. Try building your budget the whole year on the yearly budget.

How to Enhance Your Wealth Today

Yearly Budget Template														
Starting Balance	$1,500												Total	Average
Total Income	$0	$0	$0	$0	$0	$0	$0	$0	$0	$0	$0	$0	$0	$0
Total Expenses	$0	$0	$0	$0	$0	$0	$0	$0	$0	$0	$0	$0	$0	$0
NET (Income - Expenses)	$0	$0	$0	$0	$0	$0	$0	$0	$0	$0	$0	$0	$0	$0
Projected End Balance	$1,500	$1,500	$1,500	$1,500	$1,500	$1,500	$1,500	$1,500	$1,500	$1,500	$1,500	$1,500		

	JAN	FEB	MAR	APR	MAY	JUN	JUL	AUG	SEP	OCT	NOV	DEC	Total	Average
INCOME														
Net Income													$0	$0
Total INCOME	$0	$0	$0	$0	$0	$0	$0	$0	$0	$0	$0	$0	$0	$0
HOME EXPENSES														
Mortgage/Rent													$0	$0
Home/ Insurance, utilities, etc.													$0	$0
Total HOME EXPENSES	$0	$0	$0	$0	$0	$0	$0	$0	$0	$0	$0	$0	$0	$0
TRANSPORTATION														
Car Payments													$0	$0
Car Insurance, gas. Etc.													$0	$0
Total TRANSPORTATION	$0	$0	$0	$0	$0	$0	$0	$0	$0	$0	$0	$0	$0	$0
HEALTH														
Health Insurance													$0	$0
Life Insurance													$0	$0
Total HEALTH	$0	$0	$0	$0	$0	$0	$0	$0	$0	$0	$0	$0	$0	$0
CHARITY/GIFTS														
Donations													$0	$0
Total CHARITY/GIFTS	$0	$0	$0	$0	$0	$0	$0	$0	$0	$0	$0	$0	$0	$0
DAILY LIVING														
Groceries													$0	$0
Clothing													$0	$0
Dining/Eating Out/etc.													$0	$0
Total DAILY LIVING	$0	$0	$0	$0	$0	$0	$0	$0	$0	$0	$0	$0	$0	$0
ENTERTAINMENT														
Movies/Theater													$0	$0
Vacation/Travel/etc.													$0	$0
Total ENTERTAINMENT	$0	$0	$0	$0	$0	$0	$0	$0	$0	$0	$0	$0	$0	$0
SAVING & INVESTING														
Emergency Fund													$0	$0
Retirement (RRSPs, GIC)													$0	$0
Education (RESP)													$0	$0
Other													$0	$0
Total SAVING & INVESTING	$0	$0	$0	$0	$0	$0	$0	$0	$0	$0	$0	$0	$0	$0
LOANS & OTHER DEBTS														
Loan/Line of Credit													$0	$0
Credit Card/Other													$0	$0
Total LOANS & OTHER DEBTS	$0	$0	$0	$0	$0	$0	$0	$0	$0	$0	$0	$0	$0	$0

43

3.5 Good Debt vs Bad Debt

Debt, for many people today, is simply a fact of life. It's the way they pay for just about everything from big-ticket items like homes and cars to daily purchases like gasoline and restaurants. At its most basic definition, debt is simply an amount of money borrowed by one party from another. Under this definition, debt sounds neither good nor bad. A closer look at the subject provides a more sophisticated way of both viewing indebtedness.

Good Debt

There's no better example of the old adage "it takes money to make money" than good debt. Good debt helps you generate income and increases your net worth. Four notable examples of good debt include:

1. Technical or College Education

Education has long been synonymous with success. In general, the more education an individual has, the greater the person's earning potential. Education also has a positive correlation with the ability to find employment opportunities. Better educated workers are more likely to be employed in good-paying jobs, and tend to have an easier time finding new opportunities should the need arise. An investment in a technical or college degree is likely to pay for itself within just a few years of the newly educated worker entering the workforce. Over the course of a lifetime, educated workers are likely to rack up a return on investment measuring in the hundreds of thousands of dollars.

2. Small Business Ownership

Making money is the whole point to starting a small business. Earning income is a primary benefit of entrepreneurship, with being your own boss is also a positive result of the endeavor. Not only can you avoid reliance on a third-party to hire you and give you a paycheck, but your earnings potential can be directly improved by your willingness to work hard. With a bit of luck, you can turn your drive and ambition into a self-sustaining enterprise and perhaps down the line, an initial public offering (IPO) that results in major wealth.

3. Real Estate

There are a variety of ways to make money in real estate. On the residential front, the simplest strategy often involves buying a house and living in it for a few decades before selling it at a profit. Residential real estate can also be used to generate income, by taking in a boarder or renting out the entire residence. Commercial real estate can also be an excellent source of cash flow and capital gains for investors.

4. Investing

Short-term investing provides an opportunity to generate income, and long-term investing may be the best opportunity most people have to generate wealth. The wide variety of available investments from traditional stocks and bonds to alternatives investments, commodities, futures and precious metals (just to name a few) provides an array of choices for just about every need and every risk tolerance.

No Guarantees

While good debt may seem like a great idea, it is important to realize that even the best ideas don't always work out as intended. A second look at those four "good debt" categories underscores the point.

The Downside of Higher Education

In and of itself, an education is not a guaranteed ticket to wealth and success. A field of study must be chosen carefully, as not all degrees and designations offer equal opportunities in the marketplace. Difficult economic conditions must also be taken into consideration, as lucrative career opportunities will be more difficult to obtain during economic downturns. Workers who are unwilling to relocate to areas where their skills are in demand, or are unwilling to accept low-paying, entry-level jobs may find their degrees don't deliver the expected returns.

The Risks of Small Business Ownership

Like any business venture, small businesses run the risk of failure. Hard work, a good game plan and a little bit of luck may all be necessary to help you fulfill the dream of working for yourself.

The Real Estate Money Pit

Until just a few years ago, buying real estate seemed like a guaranteed win for most homeowners, as price appreciation over time was more the norm than not in good neighborhoods. Downward fluctuations in real estate prices have taught many homeowners that price appreciation is not guaranteed. On the other hand, real estate taxes and home maintenance costs last forever.

Investing

Investing can be a complex and volatile process. Just as fortunes can be made, they can also be lost. Do-it-yourself investing isn't the right path for all investors, and even hiring help doesn't guarantee a positive result.

Bad Debt

While even "good debt" can have a downside, certain debts are downright bad. Items that fit into this category include all debts incurred to purchase depreciating assets. In other words, "if it won't go up in value or generate income, you shouldn't go into debt to buy it." Some particularly notable items related to bad debt include:

1. Cars

Vehicles are expensive. New cars, in particular, cost a lot of money. While you may need a vehicle to get yourself to work and to run the errands that make up everyday life, paying interest on a car is simply a waste of money. By the time you leave the car lot, the vehicle is already worth less than it was when you bought it. Put your ego aside and pay cash for a used car, if you can afford to do so. If you can't, buy the least expensive reliable vehicle you can find and pay it off as quickly as you can. Buyers who insist on living beyond their means and financing a new car should look for a loan with little to no interest on it. While you'll still be spending a large amount of money for something that eventually depreciates until it is worthless, at least you won't be paying interest on it.

2. Clothes, Consumables and Other Goods and Services

It's often said that clothes are worth less than half of what consumers pay to purchase them. If you look around a used clothing store, you'll see that "half" is being generous. In addition to clothing, vacations, fast food, groceries and gasoline, these are all items commonly bought with borrowed money. Every penny spent in interest on these items is money that could have been used more wisely elsewhere.

3. Credit Cards

Credit cards are one of the worst forms of bad debt. The interest rates charged are often significantly higher than the rates on consumer loans and the payment schedules are arranged to maximize costs for the consumer. Keeping a balance on a credit card is rarely a good idea.

The Gray Area

In between good debt and bad debt is a gray area that generates a lot of controversy. Three hot button topics in this realm include:

Consolidation Loans

For consumers who are already in debt, consolidating higher-interest debt by taking out a loan at a lower rate of interest is a great idea, in theory. In reality, it often just frees up cash flow that consumers use to fund new debt.

Borrowing to Invest

Leveraging, or borrowing money at a low interest rate and investing at a higher rate of return (most likely with a margin account), may appear to investors as a solid way to receive better than expected results. Unfortunately, with it come numerous risks for the inexperienced and the potential hazard of losing a significant amount of money and being required to compensate your broker for the borrowed funds used in trading.

Credit Card Reward Programs

There are some great credit card reward programs available for consumers. The money spent using credit cards can help buyers earn free airline tickets, free cruises, cash back and a host of other benefits. The danger here is that the interest spent on the credit card debt offsets the value of the rewards.

Conclusion

There is certainly an argument to be made that no debt is good debt. Unfortunately, few people can afford to pay cash for everything they purchase. With that in mind, a motto of "everything in moderation" is the right approach to take where debt is concerned. Remember, even "good" debt has a potentially bad downside.[4]

3.6 Types of Investments

One big difference between saving and investing is that investing always involves risk. If the value of your investment goes up, you could earn more than you would in a savings account. But if the value goes down, you could lose some or even all of your money. That's why you should never invest money that you can't afford to lose. There is a huge list of options for investments and I would encourage you to ask your financial advisor before making a decision on your investment portfolio. The options mentioned below are only a reference.

Mutual Funds

A mutual fund is a professionally managed collection of money from a group of investors. Instead of deciding for yourself what stocks or bonds to buy, a mutual fund manager makes these decisions for everyone in the group — deciding what to buy or sell, and when. Some mutual funds will be higher risk than others, and no mutual fund is a sure thing.

Because a mutual fund invests in a variety of stocks, bonds, and/or other products, there is usually greater potential reward than many low-risk investments, and usually less risk than buying individual assets.

Exchange Traded Funds (ETFs)

Similar to mutual funds, exchange traded funds (ETFs) are open-end investment funds that hold a basket of securities. There are a variety of investment options. ETFs can engage in active management and alternative investment strategies but for our purposes, we will focus on the more traditional style ETFs that are designed to copy the performance of a specific index.

Stocks

Investing in stocks is risky because their value can change from day to day. But, stocks can also have great potential for growth and total return. When you invest in stocks, you're investing in businesses. These could be small, medium, or large companies in the Canada, U.S., or around the world. Buying stock gives you part ownership in a company.

When investing in stocks, make sure your portfolio is diversified across different market sectors, industries, and geographies (countries). The fewer stocks you own, the more potential risk you are taking. For that reason, many investors prefer to invest in the stock market through mutual funds.

Stocks are usually bought and sold in units called shares. A share's value, or share price, rises and falls based on how much people will pay for a share. People will pay money for the stock if they think the company will be successful. If it is, its stock will increase in value. Sometimes the company will also pay its investors a dividend. That's when the company pays the shareholders a part of its profits.

Bonds

Corporations, governments and municipalities issue bonds to raise funds. In return they typically repay the bond owners with interest. In this way, a bond is like a loan. When you purchase a bond, you are lending money to a corporation or to the government for a certain period of time called a term. The bond certificate is a promise from the corporation or government that they will repay you on a specific date, usually with a fixed rate of interest.

Bonds are considered "fixed income investments" in that most pay periodic interest and principal at maturity. Bonds may provide a regular income stream or diversify a portfolio.

Interest rates are the most important factor affecting a bond's value. When interest rates fall, the value of existing bonds rises because their fixed interest rates are more attractive in the market. When interest rates rise, the value of existing bonds drops because their fixed interest rates are less attractive in the market.

Like all investments, bonds involve risk. Government bonds are at a lower risk of default, because they are backed by the U.S. government. However, their values can fall and rise based on the direction of interest rates, and if you sell them before they mature, you may potentially lose a portion of your initial investment.

Money Market Securities

Money market securities are fixed income investments that typically have a maturity of under a year. The short maturity makes money market securities very liquid, which means they can be converted into cash very quickly and easily.

The price of money market securities does not fluctuate a great deal. This fact, added to the short maturity of the securities makes them a relatively stable and safe investment.

Money market securities meet the investment objectives of safety of principal and stable income. They are also very low-risk investments.

Types of Money Market Securities

There are several types of money market securities. Each type of security involves a different level of risk and corresponding level of return.

Generally, investments with higher levels of risk compensate investors with the potential for higher return – why else would a rational investor choose a higher risk investment?

There are four different types of money market securities, as follows:

- treasury bills
- provincial and municipal short-term papers
- bankers' acceptances
- commercial papers

Money Market Securities Risk and Return Spectrum

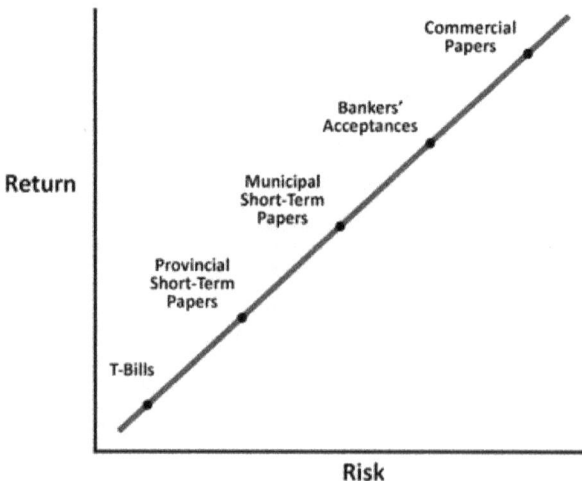

Real State

Many people invest in real estate, such as property or real estate investment trusts (REITs). One positive aspect to investing in real estate is that it has the potential to increase in value over time. Like stocks, you earn money when you sell real estate for more than what you paid for it. Keep in mind that it can take time to sell a property, and that there are costs involved in buying, selling, and owning real estate.

REITs, in contrast, trade on the financial markets. You can buy a REIT in the same way you can buy a stock. There are many different types of REITs and they offer exposure to types of property investment such as apartments and shopping malls. As with all investments, REITs can be risky — do your homework if you are considering adding them to your portfolio.

Investment Risk and Return

The chart below depicts the risk-return relationship for the different building blocks of mutual funds. Investments that are lower risk offer lower returns. Investments that offer higher potential return also come with greater risk.

Investments that experience higher volatility generally have the potential for higher returns due to the dramatic changes in the price of the investment. However, price volatility includes both upward and downward price movements. Therefore, while higher volatility provides potential for larger return, it also comes with the risk of steeper losses.

Efficient Frontier

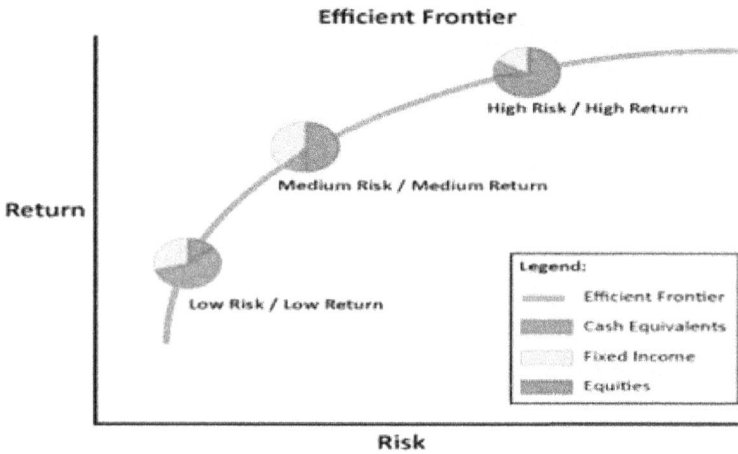

How Tactical Asset Allocation Funds Work

How Tactical Asset Allocation Funds Work

Tactical asset allocation funds are also referred to as asset allocation funds. The investment objective is long-term capital growth and income.

While balanced funds must stay within a set asset mix, tactical asset allocation funds generally have no restrictions on the allocation of assets within the portfolio. The portfolio manager has the flexibility to change the asset allocation of the fund to adjust to changing market conditions and economic forecasts. For instance, the portfolio manager can change the asset allocation from 65% equities, 35% bonds, and 5% cash to 80% equities, 15% bonds, and 5% cash.

3.7 Inflation and Interest Rate Risk

There are six main types of risk associated with investing in bonds.

Inflation Risk

Also known as purchasing power risk, inflation risk arises when the return of your investments does not keep up with the inflation rate, representing the increase in the costs of goods and services.

As a result, the purchasing power of the bondholder's coupon payments is eroded. The dollar value of your investments will buy fewer goods, because general prices have gone up.

Here's an example. When inflation rises, the purchasing power of money declines. For example, if the inflation rate is 2% annually, then a $100 purchase might cost $102 a year later.

This graph shows how inflation affects your money over time.

Decline in Purchasing Power Over Time
What will $1,000 today look like tomorrow?

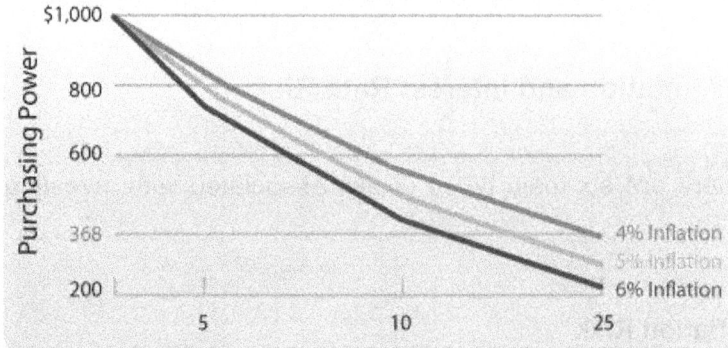

It's important to understand that if your money isn't growing at a rate at least equal to the rate of inflation, you're losing money. Try to make sure that your money is always growing at a higher rate than the rate of inflation. Saving and investing money can help you do that.

3.8 How to build wealth[5]

The wealth-building pyramid. How to get started with building wealth

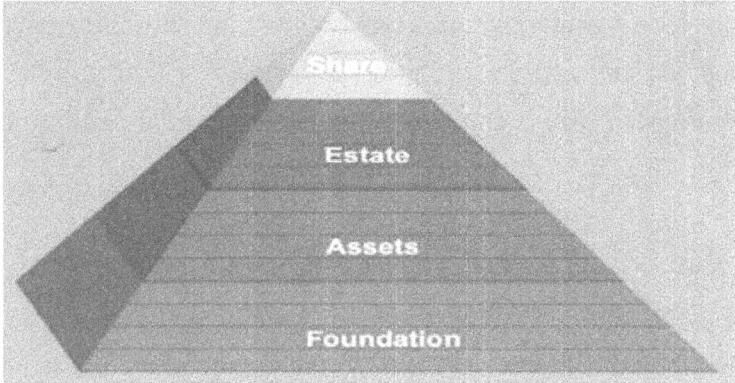

Foundation

The foundation layer is cash flow. Before someone can truly begin building wealth, he or she must consistently generate enough income to handle month-to-month expenses. It's also a good idea to have enough savings set aside to cover at least three to six months of living expenses, in case of a financial emergency. You learned the basics in the budget section of this chapter.

Assets

Once the cash flow foundation is in place, you can begin to invest in assets — investments, such as real estate or stocks. To build wealth, the value of what you own (assets) needs to be more than the amount you owe to others (liabilities). Investing in assets that appreciate (go up in value) over time can allow you to retire with a comfortable lifestyle at some point in the future.

Estate

The next layer is your estate, the wealth you'll pass on to your family and other beneficiaries. If you're a business owner, this could include your business.

Share

At the pinnacle of the pyramid are your legacy goals, or your philanthropic goals — the many positive ways you might share your wealth by giving back to your community.

Note: Remember that your wealth-building pyramid needs a solid foundation — a foundation you provide by being a good money manager, establishing credit, and managing your finances wisely.

3.9 Insurance

Protect yourself with insurance. Once you start building wealth, take steps to protect it.

Insurance can help you protect your assets. If you own a home, it is a good idea to purchase homeowner's insurance to protect your home's structure and belongings from damage. If you are a renter, renter's insurance can protect your belongings in case or theft or fire damage. Consult with an insurance professional for more information.

"If you're young and in good health, you may be tempted to "save money" by not buying health insurance. But with today's high costs of medical care, taking your chances that you'll stay healthy is a strategy that may have serious financial consequences. One serious illness can be financially devastating to you and your family. Keep in mind that the younger and healthier you are when buying a health insurance policy, the less expensive it's likely to be.

When you or your family experience a life change, make sure you review your insurance coverage, including your life insurance. While its primary purpose is to ease the financial burden of an untimely death, it can be an effective tool for both asset protection and wealth accumulation. Some types of life insurance can be used as a source of retirement income or to fund a child's education. Read about life insurance, and consult a professional to learn more.

Before you buy:

Always check the "financial strength rating" of an insurance company. This measures their financial soundness and how capable they are of handling the claims of their customers. The highest rating is AAA, followed by AA. Avoid companies without at least an A rating. The most reputable insurers receive consistently high ratings from all of these companies.

Ask insurance professionals to determine how much coverage and the types of coverage you need. A general rule of smart money management is to never insure something you can afford to pay for yourself.

Chapter 4

Defining Your Goals

Many people feel as if they're adrift in the world. They work hard, but they don't seem to get anywhere worthwhile.

A key reason that they feel this way is that they haven't spent enough time thinking about what they want from life, and haven't set themselves formal goals. After all, would you set out on a major journey with no real idea of your destination? Probably not!

Goal setting is a powerful process for thinking about your ideal future, and for motivating yourself to turn your vision of this future into reality.

The process of setting goals helps you choose where you want to go in life. By knowing precisely what you want to achieve, you know where you have to concentrate your efforts. You'll also quickly spot the distractions that can, so easily, lead you astray.

4.1 Why Set Goals?

Top-level athletes, successful business-people and achievers in all fields all set goals. Setting goals gives you long-term vision and short-term motivation. It focuses your acquisition of knowledge, and helps you to organize your time and your resources so that you can make the very most of your life.

By setting sharp, clearly defined goals, you can measure and take pride in the achievement of those goals, and you'll see forward progress in what might previously have seemed a long pointless grind. You will also raise your self-confidence, as you recognize your own ability and competence in achieving the goals that you've set.

4.2 Starting to Set Personal Goals

You set your goals on a number of levels:

First you create your "big picture" of what you want to do with your life (or over, say, the next 10 years), and identify the large-scale goals that you want to achieve.

Then, you break these down into the smaller and smaller targets that you must hit to reach your lifetime goals.

Finally, once you have your plan, you start working on it to achieve these goals.

This is why we start the process of setting goals by looking at your lifetime goals. Then, we work down to the things that you can do in, say, the next five years, then next year, next month, next week, and today, to start moving towards them.

4.3 Setting Lifetime Goals

The first step in setting personal goals is to consider what you want to achieve in your lifetime (or at least, by a significant and distant age in the future). Setting lifetime goals gives you the overall perspective that shapes all other aspects of your decision making.

To give a broad, balanced coverage of all important areas in your life, try to set goals in some of the following categories (or in other categories of your own, where these are important to you):

Career – What level do you want to reach in your career, or what do you want to achieve?

Financial – How much do you want to earn, by what stage? How is this related to your career goals?

Education – Is there any knowledge you want to acquire in particular? What information and skills will you need to have in order to achieve other goals?

Family – Do you want to be a parent? If so, how are you going to be a good parent? How do you want to be seen by a partner or by members of your extended family?

Artistic – Do you want to achieve any artistic goals?

Attitude – Is any part of your mindset holding you back? Is there any part of the way that you behave that upsets you? (If so, set a goal to improve your behaviour or find a solution to the problem.)

Physical – Are there any athletic goals that you want to achieve, or do you want good health deep into old age? What steps are you going to take to achieve this?

Pleasure – How do you want to enjoy yourself? (You should ensure that some of your life is for you!)

Public Service – Do you want to make the world a better place? If so, how?

Spend some time brainstorming these things, and then select one or more goals in each category that best reflect what you want to do. Then consider trimming again so that you have a small number of really significant goals that you can focus on.

As you do this, make sure that the goals that you have set are ones that you genuinely want to achieve, not ones that your parents, family, or employers might want. (If you have a partner, you probably want to consider what he or she wants – however, make sure that you also remain true to yourself!)

4.4 Setting Small Goals

Once you have set your lifetime goals, set a five-year plan of smaller goals that you need to complete if you are to reach your lifetime plan.

Then create a one-year plan, six-month plan, and a one-month plan of progressively smaller goals that you should reach to achieve your lifetime goals. Each of these should be based on the previous plan.

At an early stage, your smaller goals might be to read books and gather information on the achievement of your higher level goals. This will help you to improve the quality and realism of your goal setting.

Finally review your plans, and make sure that they fit the way in which you want to live your life.

4.5 Staying on Course

Once you've decided on your first set of goals, keep the process going by reviewing and updating your To-Do List on a daily basis. Periodically review the longer term plans, and modify them to reflect your changing priorities and experience. (A good way of doing this is to schedule regular, repeating reviews using a computer-based diary.)

4.6 SMART Goals[6]

A useful way of making goals more powerful is to use the SMART. While there are plenty of variants (some of which we've included in parenthesis), SMART usually stands for:

S – Specific (or Significant).
M – Measurable (or Meaningful).
A – Attainable (or Action-Oriented).
R – Relevant (or Rewarding).
T – Time-bound (or Trackable).

For example, instead of having "to sail around the world" as a goal, it's more powerful to use the SMART goal "to reduce my expenses by 10% by December 31, 2015." Obviously, this will only be attainable if a lot of preparation has been completed beforehand!

4.7 Further Tips for Setting Your Goals

The following broad guidelines will help you to set effective, achievable goals:

State each goal as a positive statement — "Execute this technique well" is a much better goal than "Don't make this stupid mistake."

Be precise – Set precise goals, putting in dates, times and amounts so that you can measure achievement. If you do this, you'll know exactly when you have achieved the goal, and can take complete satisfaction from having achieved it.

Set priorities – When you have several goals, give each a priority. This helps you to avoid feeling overwhelmed by having too many goals, and helps to direct your attention to the most important ones.

Write goals down – This crystallizes them and gives them more force.

Keep operational goals small – Keep the low-level goals that you're working towards small and achievable. If a goal is too large, then it can seem that you are not making progress towards it. Keeping goals small and incremental gives more opportunities for reward.

Set performance goals, not outcome goals – You should take care to set goals over which you have as much control as possible. It can be quite dispiriting to fail to achieve a personal goal for reasons beyond your control!

Set realistic goals – It's important to set goals that you can achieve. All sorts of people (for example, employers, parents, media, or society) can set unrealistic goals for you. They will often do this in ignorance of your own desires and ambitions.

It's also possible to set goals that are too difficult because you might not appreciate either the obstacles in the way, or understand quite how much skill you need to develop to achieve a particular level of performance.

4.8 Achieving Goals

When you've achieved a goal, take the time to enjoy the satisfaction of having done so. Absorb the implications of the goal achievement, and observe the progress that you've made towards other goals.

If the goal was a significant one, reward yourself appropriately. All of this helps you build the self-confidence you deserve.

With the experience of having achieved this goal, review the rest of your goal plans:

If you achieved the goal too easily, make your next goal harder. If the goal took a dispiriting length of time to achieve, make the next goal a little easier.

If you learned something that would lead you to change other goals, do so.

If you noticed a deficit in your skills despite achieving the goal, decide whether to set goals to fix this.

4.9 Personal Mission Statements

One of the most important things that corporate leaders do is define their organization's purpose, and identify what they ultimately want it to accomplish. They communicate this information in corporate mission and vision statements. These set a clear course for the organization, tell employees how they should focus their efforts, and prevent people going "off mission." If mission and vision statements are so important to organizations, why don't we spend any time creating them for ourselves? All of us have very different ideas about success. What's important, however, is that you spend time defining your version of success. Otherwise, how will you understand what you should be working toward, and how will you know if your decisions are helping you move toward your goals?

4.10 Mission Versus Vision

So, what's the difference between a mission statement and a vision statement?

Mission statement – This defines your purpose. It's what you ultimately want to achieve in your life or career, expressed in a specific, measurable way.
Vision statement – This is a bit more emotional. Here, you define your core values, and how you'll apply those values to your mission.

As your career develops, your goals and objectives are likely to change too. So make sure you revisit your mission and vision statements regularly, and update them as required.

Chapter 5

Neuro-Linguistic Programming

5.1 What is NLP?

NLP stands for Neuro-Linguistic Programming, a name that encompasses the three most influential components involved in producing human experience: neurology, language and programming. The neurological system regulates how our bodies function, language determines how we interface and communicate with other people, and our programming determines the kinds of models of the world we create. Neuro-Linguistic Programming describes the fundamental dynamics between mind (neuro) and language (linguistic) and how their interplay affects our body and behaviour (programming).

NLP was originated by John Grinder (whose background was in linguistics) and Richard Bandler (whose background was in mathematics and gestalt therapy) for the purpose of making explicit models of human excellence. Their first work The Structure of Magic Vol. I & II (1975, 1976) identified the verbal and behavioural patterns of therapists Fritz Perls (the creator of gestalt therapy) and Virginia Satir (internationally renowned family therapist). Their next work, Patterns of the Hypnotic Techniques of Milton H. Erickson, M.D. Vol. I & II (1975, 1976), examined the verbal and behavioural patterns of Milton Erickson, founder of the American Society of Clinical Hypnosis and one of the most widely acknowledged and clinically successful psychiatrists of our times.

Most schools on NLP have 7 principles to teach NLP, as follows. I would encourage you to take some formal training on NLP. This may help you to understand and apply the tool in your day-to-day interactions.

5.2 Communicating with others

- Build Great relationships – How to have great relationships, how to value your close relationships and keep them fresh and stimulating
- Anchors in relationships – Negative anchors and your close relationships
- Calibrated loops – a special form of un-useful anchor that can seriously damage close relationships.
- Good intentions aren't good enough – recognising and utilising non-verbal feedback

- Talking at people – or influencing them: the difference between 'old school' influencing and effective influencing is… being prepared to listen to them first

5.3 Managing your emotions

This helps you to explore how you can use NLP in managing your thinking, your moods, and your reactions to people and to situations such as:

- Physical ways to feel good
- Be more flexible: to develop your ability to be more flexible in how you handle situations
- How to have more energy and vitality in your daily life
- Personal development and Emotional Intelligence
- Anger – The Anger Habit How to understand and begin dealing with your 'short fuse' habit.
- Beliefs – Health, Beliefs & hypnosis… What we expect or believe can affect our health
- Cause & Effect
- Emotional log-jams – Learn to live in day-tight compartments
- Fear paralysis – Too much thinking can inhibit action and analysing can be hinder action and lead to paralysis by analysis.

5.4 NLP at work and in your career

NLP in managing, leading and career development

- Work and business – All your eggs in one basket – the risks of being dependent on too few sources
- Handle the Job Interview with NLP skill – how to proactively manage your interview
- Professional presentation skills are critical: NLP how to present with impact
- A key concept in team development: None of us is as smart as all of us – how a team can be smarter that the individuals who are part of it
- Thinking or doing? 'Let's talk about it' versus 'Let's get started'

5.5 NLP and Dreams

One of the areas where NLP is especially valuable is examining the connection between:

Our Dreams
Our Goals
Our Action Plans (or lack of them) …and
Actually getting around to doing something to turn the Dream into Reality.

Have a goal to make the dream a reality

To move beyond the wishful thinking we need to do something to your dream – you need to give it a reality check. We need to 'qualify it' i.e. put it to a reality test. You need to find out if it's possible to achieve it – or if you'll just keep it as a nice fluffy feel-good daydream.

5.6 NLP: Decide what you do want

What you do want is quite different to what you don't want. And it's not just about playing with words, either. Wording it positively creates a quite different mental image – and a more motivating one. For example, focusing on becoming healthier is very different to focusing on not being unhealthy.

5.7 NLP: Make sure you can achieve it – on your own

If your goal needs other people to change or to act in some way then it's just a dream, because you are not in control of the result.

5.8 NLP: Know why you want this

You must know why you want it. The more of these 'Whys' you have the more likely you are to remain motivated and to achieve your goal.

5.9 NLP: List your action steps

A lot of people don't get this far. They write down their dream and carefully qualify it so that it's turned into a goal. But that's as far as they go.

Their goal looks and feels realistic and achievable. So they relax and wait for things to happen. But nothing is going to happen because they don't have a 'to do' list to guide them in taking action! They have simply ended up with a more precise version of their dream!

The Action Steps, just like any 'to do' list, need to detail what to do first, next, next, and so on.

And they work better if they are written, too, so that you can cross each step off as you achieve it.

5.10 NLP: Take Action!

Interestingly, a lot of people take things no further than this stage.

Why? Well, the first 4 stages are comfortable. They are intellectual rather than physical. They involve mentally doing things on paper or on screen. But this is not taking action – it is preparation for action.

Planning is essential – but it must be followed by doing things – by taking action. But it is easy to delude ourselves that preparation is all we need to do.[7]

Tip: One reason why some people don't move from planning to doing is that they are put off by their goals appearing too daunting. After the initial excitement of designing the goal many people give up: 'It's too big, I'd never be able to achieve that. It'll take forever!'

This is where the little-and-often rule applies.

You need to break down the goal into tiny little steps which engage you every day or so. In this way you are not focusing on achieving the great goal: you are simply aiming for the next step.

Chapter 6

Retirement

Many Canadians share the investment goal of having a comfortable retirement. Most of us expect to retire at age 65 or earlier, with enough post-retirement income to maintain the standard of living we enjoyed before leaving our job. To do that we must develop an investment strategy that allows us to have enough money at retirement to generate the income needed to finance our retirement lifestyle.

Graphically, a retirement strategy can include some of the following elements for retirement income benefits:

Government sponsored Retirement Programs

Employer-sponsored Pension Plans

Retirement

RRSPs

Other Savings and Assets

6.1 Government-Sponsored Retirement Programs

There are two main government-sponsored programs that can help finance retirement:

- Old Age Security (OAS)
- Canada Pension Plan (CPP)/Québec Pension Plan (QPP)

Old Age Security (OAS) Program

The Old Age Security program includes four public pension benefits:

- the Old Age Security (OAS) pension
- the Guaranteed Income Supplement (GIS)
- the Allowance
- the Allowance for the Survivor

The benefits paid by the federal government through each of these programs are funded by general tax revenues. In other words, there is no contribution requirement for individuals to qualify for OAS benefits. The only qualifying criteria are age and a residency requirement. OAS program benefits are indexed every quarter for increases in the cost of living. OAS program benefits are not paid automatically to eligible recipients when they turn 65. If you are eligible for OAS program benefits, you must apply.

All OAS program benefits are subject to a "means test." If your income exceeds a certain minimum, your OAS program benefits will be reduced, or "clawed back."

The OAS pension is a monthly pension payment payable to eligible individuals. To be eligible, a person must:

• be 65 or older
• be a Canadian citizen or legal resident of Canada at the time of application approval

OR

• if the person no longer lives in Canada (a non-resident), he or she was a Canadian citizen or legal resident of Canada on the day preceding the day of departure from Canada
• have lived in Canada for a minimum of 10 years (or 20 years for non-residents) after reaching age 18

Individuals who have lived in Canada for 40 years after the age of 18 are eligible for 100% of the OAS pension benefit. Those who have lived in Canada for fewer than 40 years after age 18 are eligible for a partial OAS pension benefit.

OAS pension benefits are considered taxable income.

Starting July 2013, OAS pension benefits could be deferred, i.e. delayed, until age 70. For every month that an individual is willing to defer benefits, the benefit is increased by 0.6% per month, up to a maximum of 36% at age 70.

Guaranteed Income Supplement (GIS)

The Guaranteed Income Supplement (GIS) is available to low-income pensioners. This benefit is payable only to individuals who qualify for the OAS pension benefit. GIS is a tax-free benefit and is paid on top of the OAS pension. Individuals who have no sources of income other than the OAS pension benefit will receive 100% of the GIS. If an individual defers his or her OAS pension benefit, the GIS benefit is also deferred for the same period of time.

GIS benefits are "means tested." As a result, GIS benefits are reduced by $1 for every $2 of base income, excluding OAS pension income.

Allowance

The Allowance provides money for low-income seniors who meet the following criteria:

- the individual's spouse or common law partner (same sex or opposite sex) receives or is eligible to receive OAS pension and GIS benefits
- he or she is between 60 and 64 years of age
- he or she is a Canadian citizen or a legal resident at the time the Allowance was approved or the last time he or she lived in Canada
- the person has lived in Canada for at least 10 years after reaching the age of 18.

The allowance stops being paid when the combined yearly income of the individual and his or her spouse, excluding OAS pension benefits, reaches $30,864. At age 65, the allowance is replaced by OAS pension and GIS benefits.

Allowance for Survivor

The Allowance for Survivor provides money for low-income seniors who meet the following criteria:

- the individual's spouse or common law partner has died and the person has not remarried or entered into a common-law partnership
- he or she is between 60 and 64 years of age
- he or she is a Canadian citizen or a legal resident at the time your Allowance for survivor was approved, or the last time

he or she lived in Canada;
- the individual has lived in Canada for at least 10 years after reaching the age of 18.

Currently, the maximum allowance for survivor is $1169.14 per month, tax-free. The allowance stops being paid when your yearly income reaches $22,464. At age 65, the allowance for survivor is replaced by OAS pension and GIS benefits.

Canada Pension Plan (CPP)

The Canada Pension Plan (CPP) is a federally-administered program designed to provide the following:

- retirement benefits
- survivor benefits
- disability benefits
- death benefits

The benefits paid through each of these programs are funded using individual contributions. In other words, a person (or his or her family) is not eligible to receive CPP program benefits unless he or she has made contributions to the program. CPP program benefits, with the exception of the death benefit, are indexed annually for increases in the cost of living. In order to receive CPP program benefits, eligible individuals must apply.

Benefits are not automatically paid once someone reaches the age of eligibility.

The CPP program is designed to replace about 25% of a person's pre-retirement earnings.

CPP is payable to all eligible Canadians except those who worked in Québec. Benefits received under the Canada Pension Plan are taxable.

Québec Pension Plan (QPP)

The Québec Pension Plan (QPP), sponsored by the Québec provincial government, provides benefits similar to those offered by the Canada Pension Plan (CPP) to workers in Québec. (The CPP does not apply in Québec.) The federal government and the Québec provincial government closely coordinate the CPP and QPP.

Benefits received under the Québec Pension Plan are taxable.

Who Contributes to CPP/QPP?

You must contribute to the CPP/QPP if you do the following:

- work in Canada
- are over 18 years of age and have pensionable employment income exceeding the year's basic exemption (YBE) of $3,500

Payments into the CPP/QPP are tax deductible for employers and a tax credit for individuals. Since 2001, self-employed individuals can deduct half of their contributions and claim a tax credit for the other half. Individuals do not make contributions if they are collecting CPP/QPP disability benefits, they are not in the workforce, or they reach age 70.

Making CPP/QPP Contributions

CPP/QPP payments are based on mandatory contributions made by workers and their employers. Self-employed individuals are required to make both the employee and the employer portions of the contribution. Contributions are calculated based on a percentage of a person's annual earnings between a minimum, known as the year's basic exemption, or YBE; and a maximum, known as the year's maximum pensionable earnings, or YMPE. For the CPP, the contribution rates are 4.95% for both the employee and employer portions of the contribution. For the QPP, the contribution rates are 5.1% for both the employee and employer portions of the contribution.

Early Collection of CPP/QPP Retirement Pension Benefits

A person may choose to collect CPP/QPP retirement pension benefits at any time between the ages of 60 and 70. It is not necessary to stop working to receive a retirement pension. Under the CPP/QPP, normal retirement is considered to begin at age 65.

If an individual chooses to start collecting his or her pension prior to age 65, the CPP/QPP pension benefit is decreased.

The maximum reduction for a person who applies for and receives their QPP retirement pension at age 60 is 0.5% per month, or 30% (60 months x 0.5 per month).

Late Collection of CPP/QPP Retirement Pension Benefits

If an individual chooses to start collecting CPP/QPP pension benefits after age 65, the pension benefit is increased. Currently the amount of the retirement pension is increased by 0.7% for every month after a person's 65th birthday until age 70. This represents a maximum increase of 42%.

CPP Disability, Survivor and Death Benefits

Disability benefits are payable to eligible CPP contributors who are no longer able to work at any job on a regular basis. The disability must be long-lasting or likely to result in death. There is also a children's benefit available for the children of individuals who receive the CPP disability benefit. Survivor benefits are paid to the estate, surviving spouse or common-law partner, and dependent children of a deceased contributor. In addition to survivor benefits, a lump sum death benefit is payable to the estate of a deceased contributor.

For individuals receiving the CPP disability benefit, when they turn 65 the benefit is automatically converted to a retirement pension. They do not need to apply.

6.2 Employer-Sponsored Registered Pension Plans (RPPs)

In order to provide employees with an additional incentive to remain with the company, many employers provide benefits designed to provide employees with a pension at retirement. Registered pension plans are registered in accordance with the pension legislation of the jurisdiction, federal or provincial, in which the plan is offered. In addition, registered pension plans must meet certain registration requirements under the Income

Tax Act, which is administered by the Canada Revenue Agency.

There are two basic types of registered pension plans:

- defined benefit pension plans
- defined contribution pension plans

Employers generally sponsor pension plans, although in some cases unions may sponsor them. The plan sponsor has the responsibility for funding the plan. An employer may make all of the contributions to a registered pension plan; although employees are often required to make contributions as well.

Investment earnings on deposits within the plan grow tax-free. However, retirement benefits are taxable to the employee when they begin to withdraw money from the plan. Employee and employer contributions are tax deductible. Registered pension plan benefits are also creditor-proof, so employees cannot lose their pension benefits if they are bankrupt.

Defined Benefit Pension Plans (DBPPs)

A DBPP defines the benefit that an individual will receive at retirement. The benefit is known and guaranteed, and is calculated based on the type of plan.

The pension plan can use the employee's average pensionable earnings as a means to calculate the benefit. Employees' average pensionable earnings will be based on one of the following:

- their earnings throughout their career with the employer
- their earnings over their final years with the employer, usually 3 or 5 years
- their best earning years with the employer, usually 3 or 5 years

Defined Contribution Pension Plans (DCPPs)

A DCPP, also known as a money purchase plan, defines the contribution that an individual and his or her employer will make each year before the employee's retirement. The amount that the employee will receive at retirement is not guaranteed and there is no retirement formula. Since the amount that the person will have at retirement depends on how well the investments are managed, the employee is often provided with the option to choose their investments from a pre-determined list of investment options.

NOTE: The current trend among employers has been to move away from DBPPs to DCPPs, since DCPPs present less risk to corporations.

6.3 Individual Pension Plans (IPPs)

An IPP is a maximum funded defined benefit pension plan usually set up by incorporated professionals, such as dentists, or by profitable corporations for their senior executives. A maximum funded IPP is one where the accrual rate is 2%. IPPs are ideally suited for individuals who are over the age of 40 and earn more than $100,000 per year. There are a number of advantages to these types of plans, including:

- annual contribution limits are higher than for other registered savings plans
- contributions are tax deductible to the corporation
- contributions can be made based on past service retroactive to 1991
- retirement benefit is known and guaranteed
- additional contributions are allowed if investment perform poorly
- investment growth is not taxed until withdrawals are made from the plan
- pension benefits are creditor proof

6.4 Deferred Profit Sharing Plans (DPSPs)

A DPSP is a plan in which an employer sets aside a portion of its profits for the benefit of some or all of its employees. Only the employer may make contributions to a DPSP. The plan can be set up such that contributions are only made when the company has a profitable year. Unlike registered pension plans, the employer is not obligated to make plan contributions every year. In addition, employer contributions are tax deductible. The employee benefits from a DPSP since the plan may be set up in addition to other registered savings plans provided by the employer. As a registered savings plan, any investment growth is tax-sheltered until the employee withdraws money from the plan.

Pension Income Splitting

TIP: Certain pension income, referred to as eligible pension income, may be split between a pensioner and his or her spouse or common-law partner. The advantage of pension income splitting is that 1/2 of the pension income that would have been taxed in the hands of the pensioner can then be taxed in the hands of the spouse or common-law partner. If the spouse or common-law partner is in a lower tax bracket, the couple will save on taxes.

Some of the types of income that a pensioner can split with his or her spouse or common-law partner when the pensioner is 65 years of age or older include:

- the taxable portion of life annuity payments
- a pension income from a DBPP or DCPP
- DPSP income
- RRSP income
- RRIF income
- regular annuity payments

When a pensioner is less than 65 years of age, these amounts can only be split with a spouse or common-law partner if received directly from a pension plan or if they were received as a result of the death of a spouse or common-law partner.

Useful Links:

Employment and Social Development Canada: Retirement Pensions
URL: esdc.gc.ca/eng/retirement/index.shtml
Québec Pension Plan
URL:
rrq.gouv.qc.ca/en/programmes/regime_rentes/Pages/regime_re
ntes.aspx
Canada Revenue Agency
URL: cra-arc.gc.ca/.

6.5 RRSP Contributions

A registered retirement savings plan (RRSP) is a type of registered savings plan set up under the Income Tax Act and registered with the Canada Revenue Agency. An RRSP is not an investment. You cannot buy an RRSP. Instead, an RRSP is a registered investment vehicle within which investors can deposit various types of investments. In order to contribute to an RRSP, an individual must have earned income.

An individual may only contribute into his or her own RRSP up until December 31 of the year in which he or she turns age 71. After that date, he or she may contribute to a spousal plan up until December 31 of the year in which the spouse turns age 71. Contributions to an RRSP may take the form of cash or in-kind (non-cash) contributions. A cash contribution is made for its cash value. On the other hand, in-kind contributions are made at their current market value. If the market value exceeds the purchase price, the investment income must be reported on the investor's tax return when the asset is transferred into the RRSP.

Deferred Profit Sharing Plans (DPSPs)

The annual RRSP contribution limit is not a straightforward calculation. In order to make it easier to determine the amount that an individual can contribute to his or her RRSP, the Canada

Revenue Agency provides each person with a notice after they have assessed that person's tax return. Among other things, this Notice of Assessment (NOA) reports the RRSP contribution limit for the tax year following the tax year to which the NOA applies.

RRSPs & Tax Deductions

Investors can deduct RRSP contributions from their total income. This reduces the amount of income tax they pay. The total income tax deduction that an individual may claim for a calendar year is determined by his or her RRSP contributions during the year and the first 60 days of the following year. Contributions made in the first 60 days of a given calendar year can be applied to the previous year rather than the year in which they were made.

Investors can also carry forward unused deductions, if they do not deduct RRSP contributions from their total income in the current year. This enables them to reduce their total income in future tax years. If you expect your income to increase significantly in the future, it may make sense to carry forward your income tax deductions.

RRSPs & Tax Deferral

The growth on money invested inside an RRSP is not subject to tax until it is withdrawn. In other words, the tax payable on investment growth is deferred until the future. Since income earned inside an RRSP is tax-sheltered, RRSP investments grow much faster than non-registered investments held outside an RRSP.

When applying tax deferral strategies, it is essential that you take into account your future tax obligations, as well as the tax savings, in order to ensure the best possible return in the long term.

Example: RRSPs and Tax Deferral

Evelyn contributes $10,000 at the beginning of each year to an RRSP account. Her brother, Scott, contributes $10,000 at the beginning of each year to a non-registered account. Evelyn and Scott each earn 8% compound interest on their investment. Since Scott is investing in a non-registered account, he will pay taxes at his marginal tax rate of 40%. The table below shows how much each of them will have saved at the end of various time periods.

At the end of...	Evelyn's Registered Account	Scott's Non-registered Account
Year 1	$10,800	$10,480
Year 5	$63,359	$57,678
Year 10	$156,455	$130,592
Year 20	$494,229	$339,296
Year 30	$1,223,459	$672,832

Since Evelyn's contributions and investment growth are not taxed until they are withdrawn, she will accumulate a greater amount over time. Evelyn's investment growth is fully re-invested and accumulates additional growth over and above her regular annual deposits of $10,000. An investment is said to compound when the growth of the investment itself is re-deposited to grow.

In addition, Evelyn will receive a tax deduction each year. For example, if Evelyn's income falls within a 40 percent marginal tax bracket, her $10,000 annual contribution will reduce her taxes payable by $4,000, calculated as $10,000 x 40%. If Evelyn has any remaining RRSP contribution room, she can invest this tax saving in her RRSP. Alternatively, she may invest this amount within a non-registered savings plan. As a result, Evelyn's RRSP contributions not only provide tax-sheltered growth, but also provide tax deductions that can be used to increase the benefits of investing within an RRSP.

Note that Evelyn's registered account will become taxable upon withdrawal. Given the higher dollar amount in her account, compared to Scott's, she will have a greater tax obligation when she begins withdrawing the funds.

TIP: Spousal RRSPs

A spousal RRSP allows one spouse to be the contributor while the other spouse is the annuitant. Historically, spousal RRSPs were set up to allow couples to split their RRSP contribution such that their income at retirement was more evenly balanced. This would have the effect of minimizing their income tax liability. The tax benefit of a spousal RRSP is maximized when the higher income spouse or common-law partner contributes to a spousal RRSP where the lower income spouse or common-law partner is the annuitant. In this case, the higher income individual is able to claim the RRSP contribution as a tax deduction. Presumably, the lower income individual, who is in a lower tax bracket, will be able to withdraw money at retirement from the spousal RRSP.

If the lower income spouse or common-law partner has RRSP contribution room, they can also contribute to a managed RRSP.

Useful Links
Service Canada
URL: servicecanada.gc.ca/eng/home.shtml
Canada Revenue Agency
URL: cra-arc.gc.ca P.

Lump Sum RRSP Withdrawals

All money withdrawn from an RRSP is subject to income tax. The Canada Revenue Agency requires that the financial institution that sponsors the RRSP apply a withholding tax before any funds are deposited into a person's bank account. As per the table below, the amount of the tax depends on the amount withdrawn and the province of residence.

Withdrawal Amount	All of Canada Except Quebec	Quebec
From $0 to $5,000	10%	21%
From $5,001 to $15,000	20%	26%
Greater than $15,000	30%	31%

RRSP Maturity Options

Investors must terminate, or convert, matured RRSP by December 31st of the year in which they turn age 71. In that year, they must choose among the following four options for their RRSPs:

- withdraw the funds as a lump sum
- purchase a registered life annuity
- purchase a registered term annuity
- transfer their RRSP funds to a registered retirement income fund (RRIF)

TIP: Recall that all money withdrawn from an RRSP is subject to income tax. If an individual takes a lump sum withdrawal of his or her entire RRSP, taxes are due immediately on the full amount. From a tax perspective, it is better to spread out the tax effect by purchasing an annuity or transferring RRSP funds to a RRIF. In addition, the options listed above are not mutually exclusive, so investors can customize their matured RRSP options to suit their lifestyle needs. Potential OAS and other benefit clawbacks should also be considered whenever making withdrawals.

6.6 Registered Annuities

A matured RRSP can be used to purchase a registered life annuity or a registered term certain annuity.

A registered life annuity provides a lifelong, steady stream of income to the annuitant, the main advantage being that the annuitant cannot outlive his or her retirement income payments. On the other hand, once an investor purchases a registered life annuity, he or she no longer has control over the investments. As a result, he or she must be prepared to make decisions with respect to the registered life annuity at the time of purchase.

The table below lists some of the decisions that the annuitant must consider.

Decision required...	Key considerations...
How frequently do I want to be paid?	Should I take payments monthly, quarterly, or some other frequency?
Should I purchase a joint-life annuity?	Does the annuity need to provide an income for me and my spouse, or just myself?
Should my annuity payments be indexed for inflation?	Does my income need to be protected against the effects of inflation? By how much does an indexed payment lower the amount that I will receive now?
For how long should my annuity payments be guaranteed, if at all?	By how much does a guarantee period of 5 to 25 years lower the amount that I will receive now?
When should I begin to receive annuity payments?	Do I have other sources of retirement income that will allow me to defer my annuity payments to the future?
How much should the joint annuitant receive after the death of the primary annuitant?	Should the joint annuitant receive 100%, 60%, or some other amount, of what the primary annuitant was receiving?

A registered term certain annuity provides a steady stream of income to the annuitant for a specified number of years. For example, a 10-year term certain annuity provides income payments for 10 years. The main disadvantage of this type of annuity is that an individual can outlive his or her retirement income payments.

6.7 Registered Retirement Income Fund (RRIF)

A registered retirement income fund (RRIF) is essentially a mirror of an RRSP. Whereas an RRSP is used to save money for retirement, a RRIF is used to withdraw the money accumulated as a retirement income payment. A RRIF can hold the same qualified investments as an RRSP. Similar to an RRSP, the growth of your investments in a RRIF is tax-sheltered and you control the investment decisions.

The major differences between an RRSP and a RRIF are that: 1) a RRIF must distribute assets in the form of a retirement income, and 2) contributions to a RRIF are not allowed.

Once an individual transfers his or her RRSP to a RRIF, he or she must withdraw a minimum amount each year. In the initial year of a RRIF, the individual is not required to withdraw a payment. He or she may delay the withdrawal until the following year. The amount of your minimum withdrawal is based on the RRIF balance as of December 31st of the previous year and the person's age. While there is no minimum age for starting a RRIF, an individual can postpone establishing one until the end of the year in which he or she turns 71. Since there is no maximum withdrawal limit, individuals are free to withdraw any amount they wish. However, RRIF payments are taxable and must be recorded as income on their income tax returns.

Death Considerations for Transfers to Annuity or RRIF

The table on page 107 highlights the main differences and similarities between annuities and RRIFs in cases of death.

	Single Life Annuity	Term Annuity	RRIF
What if I die before reaching my life expectancy?	If you die before the end of your guarantee period, payments continue to your estate; otherwise, payments stop.	If you die before the end of the term, a lump sum payment will be made to your estate.	The before-tax value of your RRIF may be rolled over to your spouse otherwise, the after-tax value of your RRIF assets transfer to your beneficiaries. Special rules may apply in the case of dependent children.
Could my spouse receive my annuity payments or RRIF assets if I die first?	Only if you specify a joint life annuity when you purchase the annuity.	Only if you die before the end of the term and you name your spouse as your beneficiary.	Yes

6.8 Locked-In RRSPs (LRSPs) and Locked-in Retirement Accounts (LIRAs)

Recall that a registered pension plan is a benefit program offered by some employers to provide their employees with a pension at retirement. However, some employees will leave their company before retirement. In this case, the employee has a number of options with respect to their registered pension plan (RPP). Employees can:

- forfeit the employer contributions, and receive their own contributions plus any investment earnings on those deposits
- leave their money in the plan and collecting a pension from the pension plan when they reach normal retirement age, often defined as age 65

In addition

- if the individual's new employer has an RPP, the employee may be able to transfer his or her money to the new employer's RPP
- if the employee is under age 55, he or she may be able to transfer the pension benefits to a locked-in RRSP (LRSP) or a locked-in retirement account (LIRA)

Employees are allowed to transfer the money they have contributed to the plan plus any investment earnings on those deposits. In addition, employees will be able to transfer the employer's deposits plus investment earnings if they have been with the employer for a certain length of time, usually two years. An employee's right to the employer's deposits and investment earnings is known as vesting. Vesting refers to the employee's right to keep any employer contributions made and investment growth earned on behalf of the employee.

Benefits from a registered pension plan must be used to provide employees with a retirement income when they reach normal retirement age, defined as age 65. LRSPs and LIRAs are similar to RRSPs, with two key differences. First, deposits to a LRSP or a LIRA can only come from a transfer of RPP assets. You cannot make regular contributions to the account types. Second, withdrawals from a LRSP or a LIRA are restricted since pension legislation requires that these account types be used for the sole purpose of providing you with an income at retirement.

Although LIRAs were introduced to replace LRSPs, LRSPs are still available in British Columbia, and federal jurisdictions. Otherwise, LIRAs and LRSPs are virtually identical in structure.

6.9 Life Income Funds (LIFs) and Locked-in Retirement Income Funds (LRIFs)

Investors must convert their LRSP or LIRA by December 31st of the year in which they turn age 71. In that year, they must choose among the following four options for their LRSPs or LIRAs:

- purchase a registered life annuity
- transfer their LRSP or LIRA funds to a life income fund (LIF)
- transfer their LRSP or LIRA funds to a locked-in retirement income fund (LRIF)
- transfer their LRSP or LRA funds to a prescribed retirement income fund (PRIF)

Recall that withdrawals from an LRSP or a LIRA are restricted since pension legislation requires that these account types be used for the sole purpose of providing you with an income at retirement. As such, most of the transfer options mentioned above include a provision that places a maximum limit on the amount that you may withdraw during a calendar year. Similar to a RRIF, the PRIF option above is the only option where you can withdraw the entire account balance at any time. In other words, registered pension plan assets that end up in a PRIF account may be cashed in.

6.10 Transfer Options LIFs, LRIFs and PRIF

The transfer option you choose depends on the provincial or federal jurisdiction within which the plan was set up. The table below provides an overview the provincial and federal jurisdictions in which each option is available.

Pension Jurisdiction	Life Annuity	LIF	LRIF	PRIF
Alberta	X	x	x	
British Columbia	X	x		
Manitoba	X	x	x	x
New Brunswick	X	x		
Newfoundland and Labrador	X	x	x	
Nova Scotia	X	x		
Ontario	X	x	x	
Prince Edward Island				
Québec	X	x		
Saskatchewan				x
Federal	X	x		

Note: PEI has no locking provision with respect to pension plans. In other words, there is no restriction placed on withdrawal amounts for pension plans that are administered according to the Pension Act in the province of PEI.

The calculation for the minimum withdrawal amount that must be made from a LIF, LRIF, or PRIF account is identical to the minimum withdrawal calculation for a non-qualifying RRIF. The maximum withdrawal amount for a LIF or LRIF is determined by the provincial or federal jurisdiction within which the plan was set up. In addition, the maximum withdrawal amount will vary according to the owner's age, current long-term interest rates, and the previous year's investment returns for the fund. In some jurisdictions, a LIF has to be converted to a life annuity at age 90.

Chapter 7

Taking Advantage of the Economic Trends

If a picture is worth a thousand words, a good chart has just as much capacity to inform our understanding of the world. In this chapter I will cover some of the most important factors and trends of the Canadian economy and give you some tips as to how you can profit from making smart investments in the economic wheel of the country.

7.1 Disposable Income

The challenge for most individuals and families is about doing more with less. As shown in the chart on page 114, the real per capita household disposable income in Ontario has decreased dramatically during the last 3 decades.

Real per capita household disposable income
Ontario/Canada ratio

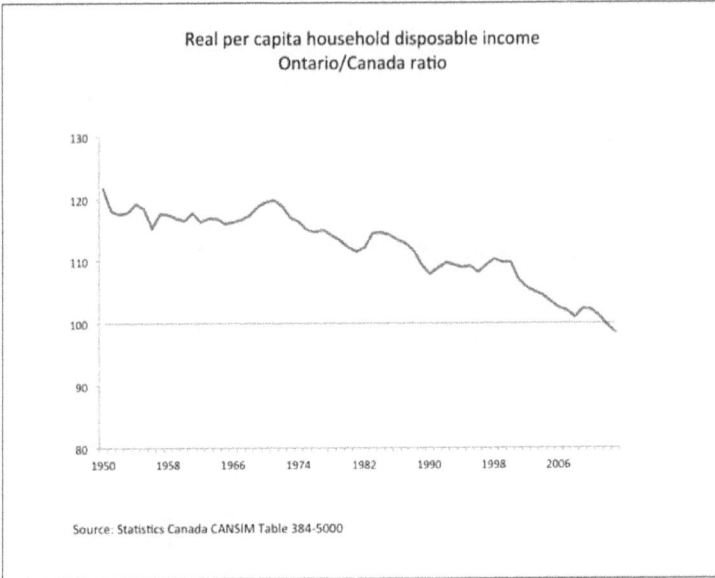

Source: Statistics Canada CANSIM Table 384-5000

"For decades, households in Ontario had incomes as much as 20 per cent above the Canada average, and 10 per cent higher as recently as the turn of the century. A steep decline over the past decade culminated in Ontario incomes falling below the national average for the first time ever in 2012. The struggling Ontario economy is a major reason why Canada seems stuck in the slow-growth lane of economics."[8]

7.2 Many households don't have financial safety nets

Frequency (%) of ownership of selected assets, by household income quintile, working-age households only

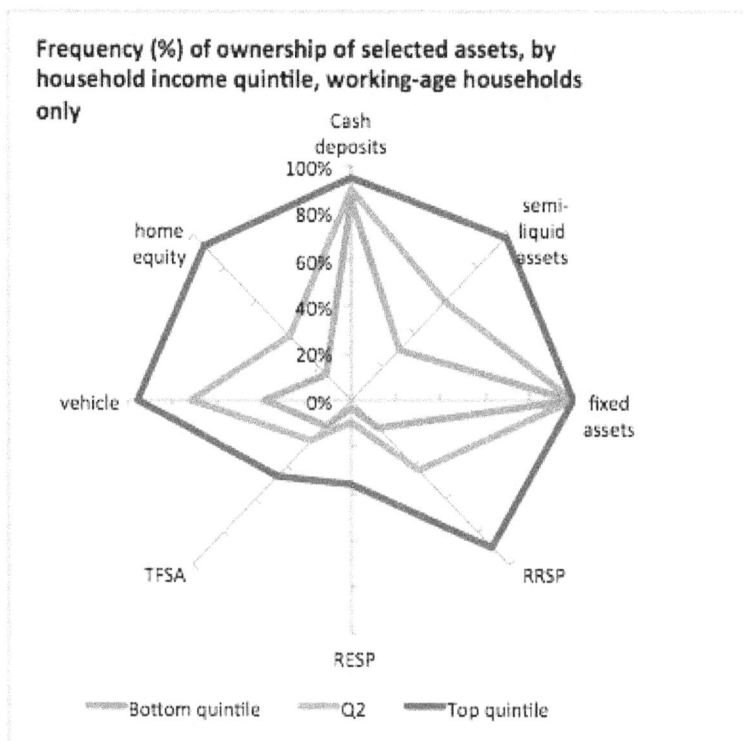

"This is a spider graph from the 2012 Survey of Financial Security (Statistics Canada) showing the incidence of ownership of certain kinds of assets by household income quintile. It's from a study I did this year commissioned by Prosper Canada. Semi-liquid assets here refers to equity in a principal residence (also broken out on its own), locked-in retirement savings and pension assets — financial assets that are imperfectly liquid. To me, this is a peek at the safety nets of households in different income groups.

The high income households have nice broad, diversified safety nets that can allow them to withstand shocks (oil prices, housing prices, employment fluctuations, unexpected illness) by shifting through short, medium and long-term forms of saving. They also are far and away more likely to have the kinds of assets (home equity, TFSAs, RRSPs) that benefit from favourable tax treatment. On the other hand, the lowest and modest income households have much narrower personal safety nets. A sudden shock can mean they quickly blow through their cash deposits and have no medium-term semi-liquid savings. To borrow the phrase from Michael Barr's book, they have no slack. Given softer economic projections and a more volatile global economic environment, we need to be paying more attention to household differences in assets and resilience."[9]

7.3 Millennials will support house prices, for now

"The chart on the following page shows yearly growth in the number of Canadians aged 25 to 34—the millennials—including Statistics Canada's projection. This cohort of prime first-time home buyers will continue to underpin housing demand for a while. So, Toronto and Vancouver's high-flying markets could remain hot in 2016, especially if interest rates stay low and foreign wealth continues to pour in. But it will likely be a different story next decade when this age group starts shrinking, as occurred in the 1990s when the baby boomers approached middle age."[10]

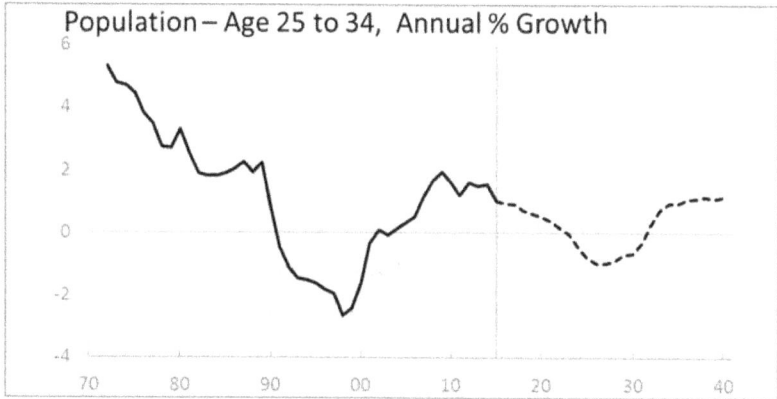

Population – Age 25 to 34, Annual % Growth

7.4 The Rule of 72 for investments

The 'Rule of 72' is a simplified way to determine how long an investment will take to double, given a fixed annual rate of interest. By dividing 72 by the annual rate of return, investors can get a rough estimate of how many years it will take for the initial investment to duplicate itself.

For example, the rule of 72 states that $10,000 invested at 8% would take 9 years ((72/8) = 9) to turn into $20,000.

When dealing with low rates of return, the rule of 72 is fairly accurate. This chart compares the numbers given by the rule of 72 and the actual number of years it takes an investment to double.

TIP: The rule of 72 works perfectly for Millennials since they have a long time horizon. Only with a TFSA investment they can build a tax free retirement fund.

Example: Pamela is 23 years old and she wants to put $20,000 on her TFSA with an expected rate of return of 8% per year every 9 years starting today and since she just finished university she expects to max out her contributions every 9 years with the current limit of $5000 per year.

The math would be as follows:

The rule of 72

Age	Year 2016	2025	2034	2043	2052
23	$ 20,000	$ 40,000	$ 80,000	$ 160,000	$ 320,000
32	$ -	$ 45,000	$ 90,000	$ 180,000	$ 360,000
41	$ -	$ -	$ 45,000	$ 90,000	$ 180,000
50	$ -	$ -	$ -	$ 45,000	$ 90,000
59	$ -	$ -	$ -	$ -	$ 45,000
Total	$ 20,000	$ 85,000	$ 215,000	$ 475,000	$ 995,000

7.5 Housing is affordable at the national level

Housing Affordability Index for Canada (Source: Bank of Canada)

"Will 2016 be the year the Canadian housing market finally collapses? This is an important question to ask not only because housing tends to be the biggest asset for most Canadians but the sector is also a major driver of booms and busts in the Canadian economy. While certain housing markets, like Vancouver and Toronto, do seem frothy and at risk of some kind of correction, the Bank of Canada's Housing Affordability Index suggests a bust is not on the horizon at the national level. As of mid-2015, the measure (see uneven line in chart) shows that less than a third of disposable income is required by a representative Canadian household for mortgage payments and utility fees–below the long term average (brown line). Side note: The affordability measures from Royal Bank of Canada show housing to be less affordable but they use posted mortgage rates whereas the Bank of Canada uses discounted mortgage rates."[11]

7.6 Buying a house – 4 Ways to boost your down-payment

With the increases of the house prices in Canada many of the young people find very hard to save money for the down-payment. As first-time buyer they can boost their down payment as follows:

1. Borrow from Mom and Dad

For many young people the down payment of their first home will be the largest amount of money they had to save. It is more common that parents support their children when buying their first home.

2. Find a side hustle to fund your goals

My wife and I decided to help our son with 20% of the value of his 2 bed + 2 bath condo down-town. Since he is renting one of the bedrooms he is paying only for 50% of the mortgage with money from his pocket.

3. Trim expensive luxuries from your budget

Small changes in your buying behaviours can make a huge difference. Instead of going out for dinner 4 times a week you can go out 2 times. Let's say you save $40 per week; that makes $2,080. A friend of mine used to smoke. The way that she quit is that for one year she put $10 bucks every day in a jar (the cost of a pack of cigarettes). She ended with $3,650 after one year. Right there you may have $5,730. If you put that money in your TFSA and apply the rule 72 you can make a lot of money.

4. Make a tax-free withdrawal from your RRSP

As first-time buyer you can make a tax-free withdrawal of up to $25,000 from your RRSPs under the Home Buyers Plan (HBP). This means a couple purchasing their first home can put together up to $50,000 towards a down payment. The money must be paid back over a period of 15 years beginning in the second year after you make the withdrawal.

7.7 The rental market remains tight in hot markets

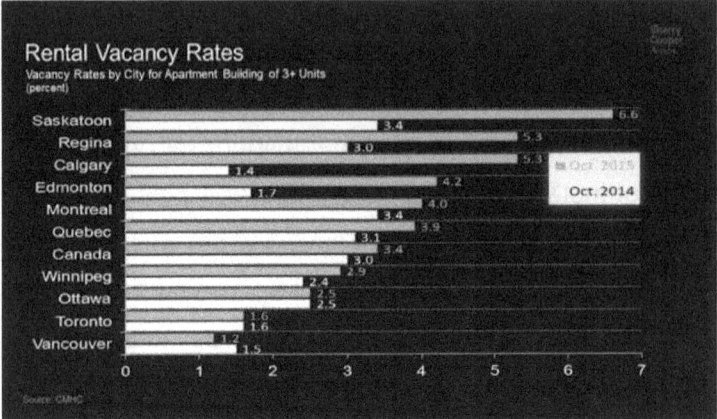

"Rental vacancy rates are a leading indicator of housing activity, especially in the condo sector. What is noteworthy about this chart is that rental vacancy rates have skyrocketed in those regions where the oil price has hit the hardest—Alberta, Saskatoon and Atlantic Canada. In these provinces housing has slowed—sales, construction and prices are down. But, note that in the hottest markets—Vancouver and Toronto—rental vacancy rates remain extremely low and even fell in Vancouver, despite huge condo construction activity. This shows that these markets are not overbuilt, although I do believe housing will slow in these two cities in 2016."[12]

7.8 Rental Property Investment

Purchasing a rental property has become a trending topic in Canada as of late. As such, it might be valuable to go over the basics of investing in rental property with confidence. Most people buy a rental property for one or all of the following reasons:

- They plan to pay off their mortgage and use the rental property as a monthly income source for when they retire a.k.a. they want to create a "Personal Rental Pension"
- They hope to create a capital gain by selling the rental property for more than they paid.
- They want to diversify their investments by purchasing a rental property; and having an asset outside of financial markets (e.g., stocks, mutual funds, GICs).

Investing in rental property has risks as any other investments. I highly recommend consulting with your financial advisor before embarking onto that journey.

TIP: Rental property is a great opportunity as an investment for retirement. Some friends say they don't have the skills to deal with tenants. I tell them that they can still make the investment an hire the services of a property manager. Property Management service providers take care pretty much of everything with a small percentage of the rental income as service fees.

Below is the analysis of the impact of investing in a rental property:

Loan Amount	$500000.00
Interest Rate	3.50 %
Years	25.00
Payment Frequency	Bi-Weekly

Interest, Principal & Extra Payments

For a $500,000 house in the GTA you put 20% down = $100,000. Your monthly mortgage is around $1,700 and you charge $1,800 per month. $1,800 x 12 months = $21,600. Assuming the price of the house remain flat you will have $500,000 in 25 years - $100,000 (down payment) = $400,000/25 years = $16,000 per year. This is a 16% rate of return per year.

7.9 The Magic of the Repayment Frequency

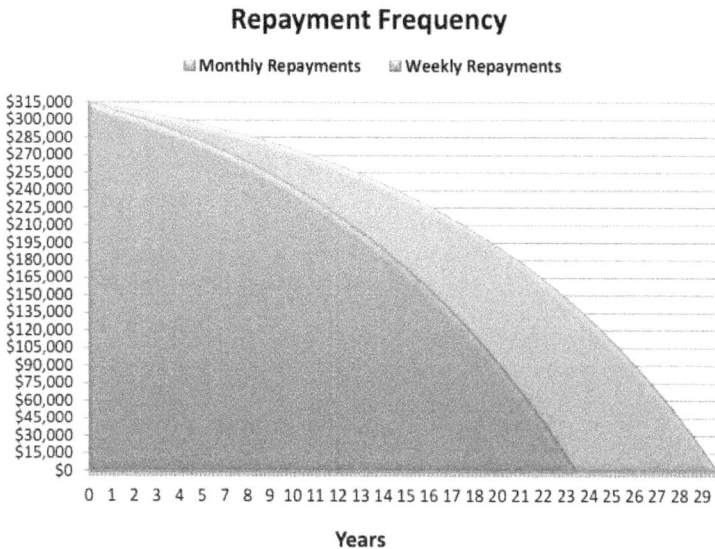

Repayment Frequency

⊠ Monthly Repayments   ⊠ Weekly Repayments

$315,000

(Years axis: 0 1 2 3 4 5 7 8 9 10 11 12 13 14 15 16 17 18 20 21 22 23 24 25 26 27 28 29)

Y-axis values: $315,000 / $300,000 / $285,000 / $270,000 / $255,000 / $240,000 / $225,000 / $210,000 / $195,000 / $180,000 / $165,000 / $150,000 / $135,000 / $120,000 / $105,000 / $90,000 / $75,000 / $60,000 / $45,000 / $30,000 / $15,000 / $0

Years

TIP: Making weekly payments will reduce the interest amount and period time by 20%. Consult with your financial advisors to discuss different scenarios.

Chapter 8

Spirituality

Often business is looked down upon by spiritualists, and spirituality is put off as non-practical by businessmen. Spirituality is the heart, business is the legs, and that is what the ancient people conceived. An individual or a society is incomplete without both these aspects. Business brings material comfort and spirituality brings mental and emotional comfort. Spirituality brings ethics and fair practice to business. In the body/mind complex depriving any one comfort means depriving both the comforts. You cannot talk spirituality to the poorest of the poor people without taking care of their basic needs. They need to be supported materially. There is no spirituality in the world that is devoid of service, and service cannot happen if material needs are ignored.

8.1 Does Spirituality Drive Success?

Executives from Silicon Valley to Boston tell how they twine their business leadership with religious and personal values. Executives from a wide range of industries trooped to Harvard

Business School to discuss how their spirituality helps them be powerful leaders.

For example, for Robert Glassman, his spirituality at work is expressed as a commitment to social justice. As co-founder and co-chairman of Wainwright Bank & Trust Company based in Boston, Glassman (HBS MBA '69) said issues such as homelessness, women's rights and outreach to the gay and lesbian community have shaped his own life and the life of his business.

Seven years ago, for instance, Wainwright Bank had a quarter of 1 percent of the commercial banking scene in the Boston-Cambridge area, but was financing over 50 percent of AIDS housing, Glassman said. In addition to outreach and socially responsible investing, the bank offers online donation functionality to any non-profit that is a bank customer—even if all they have is a checking account.

The "harmony" among his personal life, business life, and philanthropy, he said, "is as close as I'm going to come to being a spiritual person." He cited with pride the fact that his daughter works with the Coalition for the Homeless in New York City. "That there is a sense of continuity in the family [is] the most authentic thing I can say about what Wainwright Bank does."

8.2 How does one's spirituality influence generosity?

For Brent Kessel, the CEO and co-founder of Abacus Wealth Partners, 20 years of yoga and meditation practice has affected everything from the firm's investment philosophy to its culture. His ability to bridge the worlds of finance and spirituality has helped him build one of the country's most interesting wealth-management firms.

Born and raised in Apartheid-era South Africa, Kessel witnessed blatant racial and economic inequalities that still resonate and fuel his empathy today. An active Acumen Fund Partner, he recently traveled to East Africa to meet with several of the social enterprises in which they invest. On his January 2013 trip, he visited one company that is enabling micro-entrepreneurs in Nairobi's slums to buy franchised toilets. By keeping it clean, they earn money to pay off the toilet, and at the same time help reduce the spread of disease. To earn additional revenue that helps keep the cost of the toilets low, the company composts the waste, transforming it into fertilizer using a new technology created in conjunction with the Gates Foundation. In addition to his work with Acumen, Kessel has sponsored two Cambodian children for many years, and has helped raise over $600,000 to help find a cure to Type 1 Diabetes, the disease one of his sons was diagnosed with in 2003.

8.3 How do spirituality and finance connect?

Finances are an important part of our lives. It brings us stability and peace of mind for our future as individuals in our society. Financially people fall under on of the following categories. I want you to place yourself into one them.

- Survival
- Stability
- Success
- Significance

Now let me ask you again. How are your finances? How is your marriage? How is your health? How is your spiritual journey? How is your daily pursuit of joy and happiness?

8.4 Survival mode

Maybe you feel like you are in Survival mode – fighting every day just to keep living. Either you claw, scratch and fight to escape from that condition or you've given up to despair and lost all hope. Nobody wants to stay in Survival mode. It's unacceptable to the individual and unacceptable to society.

8.5 Stability mode

I think like most people, you'll find yourself in Stability mode in most areas of life. The vast majority of people in industrialized countries live in a state of Stability, because that is the lowest acceptable level, not just for yourself but for society. The trap, though, is that once your life is in a state of Stability, there is no pressing need to keep fighting to climb higher. Only a small percentage of people take advantage of their blessings, their skills, their opportunities to move from Stability to Success. These are the go-getters, the achievers. And unfortunately they are rare. Even rarer still are those that seek to move into the level of Significance.

Most people do not seek out success principles to apply to their life because their lives are Stable. They are comfortable. They will not take any action to improve their life until after they are hit by some adversity that threatens to drop them back to Survival mode.

8.6 Success mode

Success overflows to people with financial prosperity but not limited to it. If you have a strong marriage, you are better able to help a friend that is struggling in his own marriage. If your marriage is only stable, you have less capacity to help. Usually the only thing you can offer is sympathy. If you have strong faith, you have a greater capacity to minister to someone that is going through their own crisis of faith. If you have a strong, positive attitude you are better equipped to bolster someone else that is depressed.

8.7 Significance mode

All things in existence go through cycles. Economies rise and fall. Technological innovations come in waves. Relationships and moods go through ups and downs. Your health can be robust and then falter. Your faith can be strong and then waiver. There is abundance, then there is drought and famine.

When you go through the low cycles, the valleys of life, through times of drought, it will either be a mere inconvenience or a life-altering tragedy. It all depends on how prepared you are.

8.8 Being proactive

It is too late to start training for a fight once you step through the ropes (or once you step into the cage, for my younger readers). It's too late to study for the test once you sit down with your blue book and your number two pencil. It's too late to gather nuts for the winter during the blizzard.

Those are frivolous examples that all of us can relate to but don't make much of an impact. Think on these situations and see if they strike an emotional chord.

It's too late to start getting your financial house in order after you've been laid off and your family is being evicted from your home.

It's too late to start exercising and eating right when you are under anesthesia and about to have open heart surgery.

8.9 Teach your children

One of the greatest gifts we can give our children is knowledge about finances. If they have a proper relationship with material things, they will be more empowered to develop a whole, healthy sense of themselves. Teach your children that money and possessions cannot make them complete. But if they are complete within themselves, they will be less likely to chase after money or spend it unwisely. Help them learn from your own financial successes and failures, and model for them careful saving, patient spending, giving to others, and planning for the future. Show them that money is not life's purpose, but a healthy appreciation for money is essential to living with purpose.

8.10 Advice for dealing with money

The most common problems people have with money are overspending and debt. One thing you can do is go ahead and buy the thing you were thinking of buying, but then come back and check in with yourself three hours later, and check in the next day and see if the promise your wanting mind made to you actually came true. How long did it take? How impermanent was it? Becoming more and more aware of the impermanence of the outer manifestations of the world is tremendously helpful with overspending and indebtedness.

For some time I wanted to have a Camaro very badly. The time came when I was able to afford a Camaro but didn't buy it. I thought, how many days in a year do we have a nice weather in Toronto, that I can really enjoy a convertible? Perhaps 10 to 20? So I'd rather rent a Camaro for a couple of days in the summer, which is way cheaper than having a Camaro in my garage.

The patterns won't change quickly. Again, it's like sports. It's a practice. Money is the same way. Another piece of advice is to make things as automatic as possible. If you're someone who's constantly late paying the bills or has a hard time saving, set up those things automatically via the Internet. The same day that your paycheck is deposited, have an automatic dollar amount transferred into your investment account. It doesn't matter how small it is; if people can do $10 or $50 a paycheck, it changes the internal wiring. Once you start saving, the internal wiring no longer feels like "I'll never have enough." It actually starts to shift to "I do have enough."

And the biggest one is finding ways to express generosity. It doesn't have to be financial, but if it is, it communicates to the unconscious that we do have enough. Because how could we possibly be sharing and helping others if we didn't have enough? A friend of mine who is retired already plays his accordion and sings at the retirement home in my town. It is amazing to see how he makes the seniors feel happy every Thursday. When I asked him why he would do that, he responded "I am wealthy of time and I enjoy playing my accordion."

Chapter 9

Conclusion
Connecting the dots…

Congratulations! Now you have the tools and concepts to "Enhance your Wealth Today." Imagine you are the CEO of a successful company (your home). With your partner (if you have one) you will define your mission and vision statements as your lighthouse for your long-term horizon. You will identify your values and goals and align them to the stage of your life. Remember that values and goals can change as priorities may change depending on the events in your life, such as marriage, having a baby, planning for a trip, children starting post-secondary education, etc. Small goals lead to great goals!

Also remember to celebrate your success!

Your staff team is formed by your lawyer, accountant, and financial advisor who will help you with your financial and tax planning. You are prepared to tailor your budget and manage it accordingly. You will be able to leverage on the economic trends and take advantage of the tax shelters and investment options in order to generate wealth faster.

With your knowledge of Neuro-Linguistic Programming you will have congruent behaviours for managing your budget and keeping it on track. And last but not least, you will find the way to leave a legacy to your loved ones and to this amazing country.

Endnotes

1. Generational differences at work, By MELISSA DITTMANN. Monitor Staff June 2005, Vol 36, No. 6

2. Defining values: Mind Tools, www.mindtools.com

3. Creating your Budget: Manage your Finances: http://personalfinance.duke.edu/

4. Good Debt Vs. Bad Debt By Lisa Smith; Investopedia

5. How to build wealth: www.handsonbanking.com

6. SMART Goals: www.mindtools.com

7. Neuro-Linguistic Programming: http://nlp-now.co.uk/make-dream-a-reality/

8. Disposable Income: Philip Cross, Macdonald-Laurier Institute

9. Many households don't have financial safety nets: Jennifer Robson, Carleton University

10. Millennials will support house prices, for now: Sal Guatieri, BMO Capital Markets

11. Housing is affordable at the national level: Larry MacDonald, Maclean's Magazine. December 9, 2015

12. The rental market remains tight in hot markets: Sherry Cooper, Sherry Cooper Associates

www.ingramcontent.com/pod-product-compliance
Lightning Source LLC
Chambersburg PA
CBHW060606200326
41521CB00007B/676